AGENDA

Family Histories

AGENDA

CONTENTS

POEMS

REVIEWS

CHOSEN BROADSHEET POETS

NOTES FOR BROADSHEET POETS

BIOGRAPHIES 145

Elizabeth Hannaford's work has been collected
and exhibited widely, including at London's
Royal Academy of Arts, Royal College of Art
and leading commercial galleries. She also
takes commissions. Her work is an attempt
to communicate visually more than the visual
experience, drawing inspiration from the natural
world and music.

For more information, CV, contact details and
to see further examples of her work, please visit
www.elizabethhannaford.com

Editorial

Welcome to this Family Histories issue of *Agenda*.

In David Constantine's immensely readable handbook, *Poetry* (OUP, 2013), peppered with intriguing examples from poets through the centuries, he analyses the writing and reading of poetry, examining what constitutes poetry and how vital it is for us in every age. He intimates that a lot of poets start with the personal, yet 'the poet must convert the personal, anecdotal and accidental into the figurative'. In other words, the personal or particular needs to transcend itself and become universal – by, for example being deeply lived and becoming anyone's experience, particularly the experience of some reader who, unlike the poet, lacks the articulacy to put such experience into the charged speech of a poem. As Constantine asserts: 'Formal shaping helps you into the figurative. You begin to see that the poem, however personal the stuff of it may be, is not itself a personal thing', while it is the 'minute particulars' of a poem that earth it to whatever form it takes and make it achieved.

Here in this 'Family Histories' issue of *Agenda*, then, many of the poems link to family, but take experiences at a special slant, with exact choice of language, so that they leave the territory of the merely personal and flourish by, in Constantine's words, 'abundantly saying the human'.

I am sure you will all agree with Constantine when he says: 'We don't want poetry to be read by a dwindling few but by an increasing many … always there to be turned to … and working wonders'. It is thanks to you, the readers, and you the contributors who testify how very unkillable poetry actually is.

In Gwyneth Lewis's *Quantum Poetics* (Newcastle/Bloodaxe Poetry Lectures, 2015), Gwyneth refers to the Catholic theologian, Jacques Maritain who, in his Mellon lectures of 1953, speaks of 'the artistic impulse in the unconscious as essentially musical'. Gwyneth continues: 'If you picture the unconscious as a musical sea, then Maritain christened the waves behind the artistic rhythm "pulsations", a cross, perhaps, between "rhythms" and "impulses"… here he is identifying something essential to poetry'. Fittingly enough, in this issue of *Agenda*, the sections are divided by Elizabeth Hannaford's musical images or 'pulsations' which accompany the poems and articles.

It is hoped, therefore, that everyone will enjoy the musical words here that continue singing long after you have left off reading.

Patricia McCarthy

Note:
In Notes for Broadsheet Poets (an ongoing series) at the end of this journal, David Kuhrt reviews David Constantine's book.

Tony Curtis

Following the Horses

At fifteen, too young to plough, he was put to harrow
With two of his father's shire horses,
Old enough and wise enough to know their own way.

Sometimes in the length of that summer
He'd even hitch a ride on the roller –
Bird song, dreaming, not a care.

That year his clenched fists on handle and reins
Chafed and blistered and calloused
Into the roughness of a man's.

Jasper and Ned made steady progress through long afternoon
To tea-time. Then over his shoulder
An approaching thunder, rumbling low and then louder

With the roar of a Wellington dragging its shadow
Over the fields that spooked both horses and boy, so he'd run
Forward to their huge, startled heads and talked them down.

The bomber skimmed over Painters Coppice, limping
Towards Hampstead Norreys, from its port engine
A pall of smoke across the trees and into the evening sky.

That night in the White Hart his father heard them say
The landing had been a close thing,
The pilot tough and skilled at twenty-three.

But Tail End Charlie, barely older than the plough-boy,
Had caught it – his shrapnelled guts held in by
The navigator's arms until the ambulance came.

Seventy years on he wonders what the ending might have been:
Air crews didn't speak of what they'd seen
Except through nods and looks and silences.

That day: the smell of turned earth, clear blue skies
Etched with dark smoke, the reek of burning oil
Silencing the birds. And the horses' wide eyes.

Wanting Choughs

The last living thing
to be seen by Mallory in '24
as the mountain squeezed his breath away
was surely a chough,
for they are recorded near the summit
by Norton and, who knows, in '53
may well have been drawn to the biscuits
hurriedly buried by Tensing Norgay,
his Buddhist offering to Everest,
as he and Hillary paused at the peak
for as long as their oxygen would allow.

Those perpetually moving beaks,
Coronation flunkies in the Himalayan abbey,
their bright legs like Elizabethan courtiers,
as Noyce saw them, choughs drawn
to the droppings of the climbers,
their tea-leaves, the spillage of their camp.

A chough: that would be a thing indeed,
that would make my year;
but each time I walk our Headland
they are nowhere to be seen.
Reported by others, a certain pair
at least, clear against Whitesheet Rock,
but the constant crosses of black
against blue and green
are always for me no more than
the common *Corvus*, crow or raven,
never the red-beaked, red legged
undisputed primal, heraldic chough.

I've seen them on the island of Skomer,
common enough and close enough
to linger in the lens, strut their flashy stuff –
polished boot-black wings and legs full-gaitered.
But here at Lydstep,
where we scattered my father and mother,
nothing.

There's bullying black-backed gulls, rock pigeons,
once a peregrine's feeding stoop,
launched from its nest scrape in the cliffs,
hunting between Smuggler's Cave and Mother Carey's Kitchen,
but the choughs of Everest and Skomer and elsewhere
are a shape in the mind and not the evening air.

Though I should want them often to appear
for friends and family
and those who never knew me
or ever read a word of mine,
but come to the headland for the sea's green heartbeat
and a sky that goes on forever,
if my ashes were emptied out here.

Claire Crowther

Heads and Reverses

I've found a treasure of no value,
a hoard of Free State
pennies, halfpennies, dropped in our pond
by my Irish mother –
I was hosting flies,
watching them strike family water,

plane our sedge and trace an emperor
across my forehead
like Cromwell's laurel on his unlaunched
half crown. We mint common
wealth in our family
republics and we don't clean coins.

There are those who'd use cola to strip
the cover of mould
but this patina's as valuable
as the pattern below
though I don't know why,
though I know as little of muck's good

as I am conscious of this fly's aims
– on the reverses,
sows, piglets, hens with futurist wings,
familiar creatures
heralding her soiled
money, my mother's, and still unspoiled.

Tintinnabulum and Gong

My father's disappointments didn't begin with early death
but they weren't borne alone.
He failed an exam
but Granny Diddo beat his headmaster with her umbrella.

His first job, pushing a machine button with his thumb – in in –
was with his father. In-
valided soon out
of the RAF, his nurse married him, forbade the factory

and propelled him into an office. Insignia makers
kept him till he matured
into CEO
of the company he then spurred into the Birmingham Mint.

In his fiftieth year when he pulled back and started dying,
he told me: *You don't know*
as a boy, that marks
can make a working life. That badges will be how you'll spend yours.

I don't think he was depressed when he said it. He was a man
with a chest of medals
he hadn't made but made
a good iconosphere. I'd half-forgotten till I wrote this.

Mike Barlow

Shadrack

The old cemetery – history's bed unmade, its jumble
of stones leaning this way and that, tipped-over vases,
waist-high kesh, the humps and ditches of disturbed land,
all the dead turned in their sleep together,
some terrible dream of mortality calling them back.

Shadrack Benbow leans sideways at fifty degrees,
tilts forward like an old gate stoop, lichened and weathered.
Shadrack. Perhaps his father was a furnaceman, his mother
much taken with The Lord in this steel-works town
of edgeless skies and unquenched thirsts.

Once *beloved husband & father*, no longer
reckoned by the living, nor greeted by the recent dead
but a soul tipped abroad now by the ground's slow quake
as if, despite its relentless lust for our bones,
the earth offers no haven for the true believer.

The man who was not my father

would have made a man of me,
spared nothing, maudlin curses
as he rolled home drunk, the random fist.
On my fifteenth birthday
he'd have set them up then set me up
with one of Lily's girls. A fast learner,
his nod on a small-hours loiter
would have seen me shinning up
through an open half-light;
or, as we left the pub, a wink
and I'd have palmed the stolen wallet
slipped my way.

I would have been a sly tyke,
mouthy git, scrapper. With my scars,
tattoos and broken teeth
I'd have been a son my mother feared for,
cool but edgy, full of plans
but short on dreams. Ask me
and *Sound*, I'd say. Ask anyone else,
they'd shake their heads. Either way
I'd be the man he'd made.
And I'd have loved him.

Josephine Balmer

Lost

Up to that point, I was still in the dark.
I was retracing steps, staring down paths
I saw as ours, not knowing she had been
ripped from us already, had slipped unseen
as she sat down to rest. We'd just spoken –
I heard her laughing, hanging up the phone –
but when next we gathered, friends, family,
one of us would be missing, tricked away.
I bargained with gods I did not worship;
I blamed, I begged ambulance men, medics.
Reaching home, I tried to put on armour,
convincing myself that they had saved her,
that they had been in time, they had, they had ...
In response there was only silence, dread.

(after Virgil, *Aeneid* 2.735-55)

Ring

The last time he had held it in his hands
was Penzance, late nineteen-fifty-five. Storms
roaring around the church had by then ebbed;
coats were being unbuttoned, wool scarves shed.
Outside, my beaming mother had just stepped
from the car, poised between one life and the next,
as the weight of a box in new best suit
became a bond, unbroken, resolute.

Tonight he twists it between taut fingers,
peering through its opened circle as if
a peephole into some new dimension
where all the days and years might not have been.
The door chimes: undertakers at the gate.
Now there's just one vow left for him to make.

Sue Davies

Cycling on Lüneburg Heath

A song sprang out of her. Beneath her red dress
bones like shank buttons studded her back.
She sang quarter notes to the rhythms of jazz,
to the glide of marshland pricked with buttercups,
and the big drum roll of pine and oak, as we
swayed and listed, my hands gripped to the sides
of the child seat, my face with nowhere else
to turn, set against the wind whipping the tops
of junipers. The clouds fell, capped the copses,
and everywhere gems – primroses and foxgloves,
lavender and gorse, the sag and drape of grasses,
her movement pulsing through the metal frame
to my green-stick limbs prickling on the steep
incline, her back bent by the weight of love.

The Dare

Legs long
as crab spiders we sat on moss
straddling the wall that ran the length of our road,

trespassing without guilt, stealing
peaches, sweet as summer's rain, bronzed
like toads asleep in splits

in brick that wept salt. Before, at home
we slipped under our mothers' warnings to keep
dresses clean and crisp, our curls like wood shavings,

and tore free in bare feet running the length of the wall
from east to west, our feet assured, gripping ivy
and rock cress. And once, when the sun ignited the limes

you said I had to jump, knees quivering by your
command – a law to which I must
submit as we stared down into the pit of blackened earth.

And before a scream shook from you – I sprung
shot from golden dust to mid-air, my life there,
for that moment held,

and nothing else.

Peter Dale

Talking the Walk

It was a dream and not a dream:
my oldest friend, respected most,
you, striding off through dark woods.
And I, not there, called to your back,
unheard or heeded. I wondered why,
when it might be, feared when it was.

We often meet to have a drink
and talk about what drives us on,
and each can often second guess
the other's take on what is what.
 – You, walking off through the dark woods
where one of us becomes a ghost.

A ghost won't haunt another ghost.
Whose shade casts dread on our old haunts?
Whose words and hours blown through a sieve?
The vacant spirit can't be laid.
Old friend, have you vanished now?
– Here I go, still talking to myself.

Transcription

Why do this, your voice over a decade dead,
transcribing this now old, long-misboxed tape,
shop-talk of how and why we did as we did,
the life in words? – And such a chore to type.

Your voice so quiet and by turns succinct
and hesitant, obscured by restaurant din.
Your wine-list check for halves. – We'd always sunk
another whole bottle. ... Just a page done.

I cannot type your voice, the traits of tone,
and your inflexional glances. So few are left,
dear friend, who heard you, who could return
cold print to voice over. Books took our life.

We blued our days in words – on living words,
we thought, and it has come to this: is – was.

Alto Rhapsody

Her music, she had a lovely alto voice
but never had a chance of rhapsody.
She sang west Wiltshire tunes, the melancholy
of villagers who'd to choose what was no choice.

Always the low registers in the war,
as if high would draw the bombers overhead.
Two hours of daylight saving, and late to bed,
I'd hear her melodies come through the floor.

Her song without words, I hear it still,
breaking in fragments through any floor or wall,
not subject to the hour or to the will,
those registers that never rose to fall.

How shall I learn her words of endless song?
They murmur their largo my whole life long.

Wendy Holborow

A Triolet of Dance

My parents always loved to dance,
when they were young and free.
Like many lovers, met by chance,
because they always loved to dance –
across the crowded floor, a glance,
that spoke their love eternally.
My parents always loved to dance,
when they were young and free.

*

Their love was loud and boldly spoken,
the years danced by so fast
and though my father's lungs were stricken
their love was loud and boldly spoken.
And then my mother's heart was broken
the day my father breathed his last.
Their love was loud and boldly spoken,
the years danced by so fast.

Nicola Daly

Nights Above The Butcher's Shop

I wanted sweetbreads and sticky figs.
He gave me a silk purse made from a sow's ear.

He wanted my shoulders robed in fox.
He liked my feet shod in the crocodile his first wife had worn.

I never asked for this hint of musk
nor the tails, paws and tusks of exotic beasts.

I didn't expect the unicorn's horn or the necklace of pig's teeth.
I requested gloves to match my purse.
I wanted something in the palest blue to match my shoes.

He gave me my gloves, figs and a silk purse.
and he clothed me in the skins of the dead.

He covered my sex in the tang of leather,
my spine in fur and my breasts in feathers.

He wanted to carve my delicate bones
so that when I looked in the mirror I wore the face of another woman.

Mara Bergman

The Baby Doll

This is where they come to rest.
Sixty thousand objects hidden here
under the museum floor: balsa wood temples

from India, peepshows and panoramas,
magic lanterns and random pewter,
costumes, soldiers, a giant turtle.

We ease a box down from its shelf and
navigate between aisles of optical instruments,
buttons and birds' nests. Ephemera.

On a table in a patch of light we lift the lid:
a baby doll dressed in a soft pink sweater
with white buttons and cuffs.

Her sleeves are empty
where her missing arms should be.
A silk ribbon holds her leggings up.

We had an unwell baby once, a baby doll,
a brother. He slipped away in hospital,
sailed to sea in a boat. We never even saw him

and there weren't any tears
but we loved him. Inherited his outfits.
Dressed other babies in them.

Nigel Prentice

The Chat

Stalking dim galleries of childhood, casing the joint,
   I push a door ajar and smell that room,
your mothballed past in my past, our double portrait:
   great-aunt, great-nephew by the fire, in a gleam
of brass horseshoes, a squirm of glowing plastic coals.
   Here you were enthroned for thirty years.
Long summer afternoons while my mother cut your grass
   I fidgeted through my role, to chat, cheer
and agree with you; awkwardly, then with bluff and blandness
   as I took on adult arts of conversation.
You had a bright downturned smile, the silkiest hair,
   lumpy hands, cheeks powdered to the pink carnation
of a baby. And a whole life creaked when you moved.
   You held audience in a wingbacked seat,
poised stiff and pristine as the Pope, while the fire
   revolved slow underworlds about our feet.
Above, in a gilt-framed flagstoned inn jovial squires
   in red toasted the hunt (you never drank),
while our anecdotal knick-knacks matched the polished coal-tongs,
   china shepherds, line of jet-black elephants
each getting smaller. In this room of tassels and pelmets
   the mild chimes of the grandfather clock
settled everything every fifteen minutes. Galling
   to a child was the cameo entrance, slick
escape of the fat cat, sleek on tinned salmon.
   You hobbled between three rooms: we saw
only two, and the door was always shut on the front room's
   chill museum. Even in spring the air
was musty, while outside a dark wall of conifers
   closed the front garden, swayed and shuddered.
At the back were rosebeds set in perfect crazy paving,
   and beyond, the old orchard, a bristling horde
of nettles, brambles, matted grass, tightening on
   a fastness where we never dared to press.
And now I can ask, after the years of our talk have ended,
   and the family gossip: what do I possess?

Roland John

Recollections Organised from Arcadia

See an old man surrounded by books useless in a digital age,
downloading memories perfected over nearly a century of careful
arrangements, the loading of perspectives, those selected losses.

What passions examined, how much knowledge acquired
then discarded as carefully as the crafted minutes were written,
annotated, indexed, cleansed before release to the unsuspecting?

How many words saved, savoured perhaps, the arcane, the forgotten?
Bring me shalloons and similar weighted words from France,
ah that dance of the intellect amongst them, their favoured rhythms.

Not when, but how to start? First memories? Family histories?
All stories clotted and partisan, the war, Wales and her dog
my great-grandmother's bad tempered white bull terrier,

the digging for victory, a garden turned over to produce.
What did we do there speaking no Welsh? My mother's isolation,
the iron gates of the Bethesda Chapel, cousins; in the distance

the glow of Cardiff burning – do I remember this? A child
of four years, how much has been imposed and yet the single plank
that bridged the stream I remember being told not to cross. I did.

First memory then one of defiance, rebellion even, how comforting
a pretence that turns the lie of reminiscence into a statement
of intent, a welcome fabrication that insinuates and consolidates

the beliefs a long life has manufactured, maintained and scrutinised
against the commonplace. These few things time has buttressed
to make a carapace against those questions long unanswered.

Interrogations of intent, meanderings of faith, the only query
of any purpose, more important than the flight from reason
so ingrained that answers are all we have, the uncertainty forgotten.

Dylan Willoughby

The State of Things

for Elena

Tears of ghosts are not found in rain
The sun does not proclaim bold happiness

I am tied to the littoral
Half-earth, half-ocean, both sides bestial enough
I stand in this tidepool as the tide draws in
I do not conjure, I have given up that pretence

You have called me both Pholus and Chiron
And I can't tell you honestly which is right
Those starless nights we spent seem so fleeting
Yet they hold me as a willing hostage
The water can have its sad victory
It will bury me with only this memory

I am so old now, I have stopped counting tides
There is no coming and going to an old man, just drift,
Sometimes perceptible movements

You asked me what is myth and I laughed
What's the difference after all these years
When in the ruins we scarcely make out
What we think has been and discard it in any event

You are myth
You can be what's left of me

To Send Far Away

I'm told she was radiant in life.
She died the day you died, your belated bride.
We performed the wedding yesterday,
Two sad photos for stand-ins, and tears
Instead of flinging rice or fireworks.
I burnt some money for you, as well,
They say it'll reach you both.

When you were younger, I'd watch you breathe
Asleep, taken by its mystery,
The keep-going of it, its origins
So unknown. Sometimes when I peeked
You'd be mouthing words to yourself, breath
Without voice, what were you saying those nights?

You took the only road out of this town
A road I hope to take pretty soon
There's an ache in my bones wasn't there before
Nothing though compared to the broken
Air I've breathed since you've been gone.

Beth Somerford

Our Perfect Children

Surprising us, into our room they crept,
my body taken over by their drug.
I dreamed them into being while we slept.

Across that fertile rubicon I stepped,
towards their tender limbs and eyes of sap.
I dreamed them into being while we slept.

My way of life and age I should accept –
the beachy days, the ballet nights, the snug.
Surprising us, into our room they crept.

The secrets of their heritage were kept,
until the bloody slip; the milky tug.
I dreamed them into being while we slept.

Then all around the counterpane they leapt,
and danced for us a honey-finders' map.
Surprising us, into our room they crept.

On thinking of their perfect forms I wept,
tho' they were nothing but a writer's shrug.
Surprising us, into our room they crept,
I dreamed them into being while we slept.

Laundry Hill

I work at the Tivoli. Every day
is wash day here. Petticoats laid
on the grass. Hands raw and dry
from the scrub and the dolly; their
backs veined like streams at the mere.
I envy the midwife's creamed fingers.

By day's end, worsted heavy, I slip
down the twitten, along cat's-creep.
Too tired for more than a touch
of my husband's shuddering grip;
his arms wiry from graft and
the burn of trawler ropes.

Dry-wombed now, at least these
days I needn't fear confinement –
the worrisome weeks in batiste
and their tatted layettes. Though
we bathed them in wine as you said,
only four of my blessings survived.

Minnie's a seamstress for ladies. She
gathers and trims with lace; traces
dark threads like slubs in the weave.
From the offcuts and scraps she
has made me a patchwork shawl –
it will be my widow's comforter.

Charles works up at Cutress' mill,
trading tales with the bakers' lads,
and accounting the prices of flour.
From the day his cries first rose
from the bassinette,
he has always smelt of yeast.

Anna worked at The Grand;
married a man from the dairy.
He circuits the buttermilk buildings
of Hove. He is good, yet she
is strung tight – like apron cords –
and her throat has a kettle's cry.

Martha, my youngest, is fair.
She will go into service in June.
In June I will lose my companion.
But for now we will wring the wet sheets,
twisted and lumped like the cord
that once bound us together.

Abegail Morley

Mayday

In the dull copper morning after he left,
her life pauses – a thought flees
mid-sentence, breath blurs between her lips –
a ship crawling home through fog.

She takes her breakfast outside
to a small forbidden patch of sun
that keels over from next door, spreads itself
on her patio like a nylon spinnaker.

When she feels she's going under she returns,
throws dishes in the sink, trails the house seams
for clean clothes, brushed hair, broad shoulders –
finds shaving foam, a blunt razor spattered

with bristles. She mouths the word *drowned*,
rinses the blades under the tap –
he dissolves – leaves without ceremony,
a deep sea fishing boat slipping harbour.

Eloped

When my pregnant sister moved over the border
I went to her room, carried out last rites on her things,
cluttered her dressing table with my stuff: *Anais Anais,*
small pouches of patchouli oil, a bottle of *Charlie*.

I laid them like a body of bones, a teenage pattern
of ribs, sternum, an Avon make-up bag for a skull,
twist of soap-on-a-rope for intestines. That night
I guarded them, hands wrapped round bed clothes,

toes rooted between mattress and footboard, breath
nuzzled in the static of nylon sheets. At dawn
when light tore through the curtains I thought
I saw her face, her mouth moving in perfect time

with mine, *Look,* she cried. *Look.* I did,
saw nothing but her empty room, me lodging
in it trying to spin my memory of her around
my mother's mouth so I wouldn't hear her crying.

Alexandra Davis

Fairer Sex

My father always liked his women blonde.
So much so it was noted down in court
that she had never been prepared to dye
her hair for him, my mother, on the day
he fought in court; his tone so keenly hurt
by her unreasoned rebuff. So she sued
him for adultery, while he claimed it was she
who'd forced him into bed with someone blonder.

My father also liked his women small
and dainty in their size three feathered heels,
their low cut blouses like blown peonies
frilling down to tiny waists, looking up at him
a foot above their golden tresses; all quiet
and eyes. She'd never been prepared to diet,
the court notes read. Meanwhile my mother shifted,
hefty in her chair, and divorced the idiot.

Tess Jolly

Dear Molly

I'm writing from the garden where I burned all your letters,
your handwriting in school-girl ink on lined A4 pages
sent by return of post or across continents.
All those things we couldn't tell our mothers,
do you remember what they were? I scattered the ashes
on the guinea-pig graves, it seemed the right thing to do.
We cried holding hands. Like donating that dress you gave me
to the charity shop because I'd got too thin - thinner
than paper you said. I wore baggy jumpers like padded
envelopes. You asked for it back, ashes are blacker than coins.
Do coins burn? And do you remember that journey to the sea
staring at each other's reflections as if we were looking
at the same frightened ghost floating over fragile fields
like a face in a photo that wasn't there when you took it?
Whole boxes of them! I wish you'd heard the flames
singing like love. Nothing's ever lost or wasted, rain
greens into leaves, a woollen thread is woven into a nest
in the garden where I burned your letters. Little Match Girl
you only heard the forest voices pecking your thoughts
to dust. I should have read them first. No one
sends letters now. We email/txt. I'm resisting Facebook
to ask mutual friends how you are. Whole boxes of them!
You've destroyed my life you said, pills hidden under
your tongue. You said I don't exist anywhere
except this hospital ward.

Interview with Robin Robertson

Robin Robertson was born in Perthshire, and was brought up on the northeast coast of Scotland where, he says, 'history, legend and myth merged cohesively in the landscape.' His early influences include the stories of Celtic and classical myth, the vernacular ballads, and folklore. He is the author of several books of poetry, including *A Painted Field* (1997), *Slow Air* (2002), *Swithering* (2006), *The Wrecking Light* (2010), and *Sailing the Forest: Selected Poems* (2014). He has translated the work of the Swedish poet Tomas Tranströmer (*The Deleted World*, 2006) and a translation of *Medea* (2008). An American reviewer has written that 'The genius of this Scots poet is for finding the sensually charged moment – in a raked northern seascape, in a sexual or gustatory encounter – and depicting it in language that is simultaneously spare and ample.' He has worked at several major London publishing houses, and has edited the work of such poets as Anne Carson, John Burnside, Seamus Deane, Geoffrey Hill, Michael Longley, Sharon Olds, and Peter Redgrove.

W S Milne: *Agenda* would like to thank you for agreeing to contribute to this 'Family Histories' issue of the magazine. I would just like to start by asking you how important you think Scottishness is as a factor in your poetry?

Robin Robertson: Though I've spent more years outside than in, Scotland was the place where I was born, where I grew up. We are, all of us, the sum of our experiences, and our first eighteen years form a sensibility, a way of looking at the world and making sense of it: a patterning – like a frown-line on the forehead – that doesn't go away.

WSM: Perhaps the sea has something to do with that. It certainly figures greatly in your work. Can you explain that?

RR: I was brought up in Aberdeen when it was still a great fishing port, so the heart of the city was the harbour. I lived in the north, in the old town, and had Seaton Park as my playground – with the River Don running through it to Balgownie and on to the Links and the long strand south to the city and the docks. Those who live on the coast know how powerfully the sea affects their lives – their external and internal weather – but it's hard to explain to everyone else. The North Sea is a volatile, implacable, irresistible force at the door, but it also carries a heavy magnetic charge, a real grandeur and glamour. Rilke could have been writing about that sea when he said: 'Beauty is nothing but the beginning of terror, which we are still just able to endure, and we are so awed because it serenely disdains to destroy us.'

WSM: *Agenda* not so long ago brought out a Special issue on Rilke where we had a translation of his poem on The North Sea, which I think brings out that very point. Can I just ask you (or what) were the early influences on your work?

RR: I still think that the landscape of my early years had the most profound effect: the mountains behind us, the sea at our face. The folk tradition was still present everywhere: the songs, stories and music, the folklore and superstitions. I read all sorts of stuff, but Yeats, Eliot, Bunting, Geoffrey Hill and, most notably, David Jones, were among the poets whose work – which I first read in my early years – chimed with something inside me. They are all poets who were interested in a rich, impacted density of thought and language leavened by a singing line. I liked Hill's wry gloss on 'Funeral Music' – his magisterial sonnet sequence about the Wars of the Roses – when he says he was 'attempting a florid grim music broken by grunts and shrieks'. I go back to all these poets (particularly late Yeats, early Hill, all of Jones) to remind myself of the difference between 'good' and 'great'.

WSM: Again, *Agenda* has been a great supporter of Hill's work over the years, as of course it has of Yeats, Eliot, Jones and Bunting too, so I can agree with that. I take it you studied Literature at University?

RR: I did, regrettably, and it seems rather pointless to me now. I should have taken Anthropology or Classics or Comparative Mythology.

WSM: There is some sense of that in the American reviewer's comment about your work pulling many cultural strands together. That prompts me to ask – has the USA been of significance in your poetic development?

RR: I'm not sure if the US has had any direct influence on the writing, but amongst the dreck and damage there's plenty of nutrition and urgency to take from the culture: the Delta blues, the embattled romanticism of American song, the films and the jazz from the late 40s to mid 50s, some of the cities, the range and scale of the landscape.

WSM: Has the practice of literary criticism and reviewing fed into your poetry in any way?

RR: I don't practise either.

WSM: Probably very wise. There are times these days, however, that it seems to take on more significance than the work itself. Do you feel that poetry is diminished in these days of digital culture, or has it become all the more vital?

RR: All serious art remains vital, regardless of popular culture's ebb and flow, but its depth and complexity (some would bluntly say 'difficulty') will always preclude popular interest. The current cultic mantras are instant 'communication', instant 'information', and instant 'choice', and we have too much of all of them. The creative consciousness craves something slower and deeper: the sustenance and engagement of the intellect and the emotions. Hill again: 'Difficult poetry is the most democratic, because you are doing your audience the honour of supposing that they are intelligent human beings'.

WSM: Can I ask you about your own compositional methods. How do you write?

RR: Like most writers I keep notebooks, and I transcribe those notes into a large bank of active material – some of which goes back twenty years or more. This is my partial, paper version of Coleridge's 'streamy well of the unconscious'. Words, phrases, lines – sometimes whole verses – will rest in this holding tank until something from my active consciousness makes the right kind of hook to draw them back to the surface. A new image or thought or interest will find a connection with something older. Once they are brought together – out in the open as it were – there is often an instant, almost erotic coupling and the poem begins. This may all strike your readers as very peculiar, but this is how, for instance, memory works: a single new thought, smell, sound or picture can trigger a whole slew of emotions and images, even real events, that were sunk very deep and apparently lost. We each have just the one sensibility, but it is an extraordinary resource.

WSM: How do you experience literary creation at that moment of writing?

RR: After the generative spark I've just described, there is usually some fast accretion as words and images start to collect, almost magnetically, around a shared interest or theme. At this point, the poem is writing itself, almost, and I'm just allowing full play to occur between my subconscious mind and the words on the page. Once the poem declares itself I can take a more active role. If you imagine the poem as a table: the table now has a top and four legs; my job now is to make it stand steady, make it strong, and make it beautiful.

Let me change the metaphor: I spend a lot of time working on the music that the words make together within the poem, trying to arrive at a tight reticulation that can only be read in the way I want it to be read. I am writing the score, if you like, using words that have their own weight and texture and significance – and choreographing the sonic and semantic dance of those words within the boundaries of the poem. What I am *after* is an achieved organic whole, and there can be no false steps, no loose ambiguities, no redundancy; which isn't to say, of course, that I ever succeed...

What I *want* – and it comes rarely – is that moment when I look down at the freshly written page and am scared, or surprised, or shaken out of myself, and I realise that I've done this. I've made this happen.

WSM: Does that affect your reaction to critics' estimation of your work?

RR: I don't write to win praise or prizes, sell books or, even, to 'communicate'. I write primarily out of curiosity. The poem goes its own way, attending to certain buried concerns and anxieties in much the same way as dreams do. The poem is an attempt to draw out hidden strands from the subconscious mind and form them into a pattern: a shape that makes some sense of all those desires and dreads. Once it's finished, it's out in the world and not really mine any more. At that point I'm delighted, of course, if a poem or a book pleases people, or if a prize should come my way, but neither communication nor external validation are the primary motives.

WSM: Editing is a large part of your life. Has editing other poets' works helped you in your own working practices?

RR: I have a full-time job looking after nearly sixty writers at Jonathan Cape. If it weren't for the generosity of my employers in allowing me some annual sabbatical leave I'm not sure how much I'd ever get written. Close editing uses some of the same space and same muscles as writing – and so, as a poet, I've chosen just about the worst career I could. That said, I still find it thrilling, after all these years, when I chance upon something fresh and exciting – or read a new manuscript from writers like Anne Enright or John Burnside, Alice Oswald or Michael Ondaatje.

WSM: As a number of critics have noticed, the Classics feature to a fair extent in your books. Can you explain this fascination?

RR: Having been raised on a diet of Celtic folk-tales and Greek mythology I have always been interested in transformation – and the creative aspect of flux, of turning (whether 'turning away' or 'turning into') has found its way into much of what I do. The process of turning may be destructive in the end, but at least it's *active*. Stasis and paralysis fill me with dread. Ovid's masterly re-telling of classic Greek myths has long fascinated me. Under the binding theme of shape-changing, he re-makes the old, familiar legends as modern dramas of casual, arbitrary violence – concentrating less on the power of the gods and more on the vulnerability of the mortals, on the mutability of the flesh. This shift in focus, two thousand years ago, makes the *Metamorphoses* seem vigorously, fiercely relevant.

The plays of Euripides, five hundred years earlier, have a similar psychological accuracy and bleak modernity. I was commissioned to produce a new translation of *Medea*, which I wanted to be a useful acting edition but, more importantly, an English version that would feel as true to the Greek as it was to the way English is spoken now. I followed this with the *Bacchae*, which is my favourite play of Euripides, with my favourite Greek god, Dionysus, who is even more Protean than Proteus.

WSM: Translation likewise (especially from Swedish sources) is of clear importance to you. How did that come about?

RR: After being away from writing for a while I often use translation as a kind of five-finger exercise to warm up the muscles; the advantage being that the subject is already provided, and all you have to do is re-build the machine to different specifications.

The Tranströmer poems happened by chance. One July, some years ago, I was on an island off the west coast of Sweden hoping to enjoy some sailing and swimming. It rained for a fortnight, and the only book in the cottage was Tomas's collected, *Samlade Dikter, 1954-1996*, so for each day of rain I worked on one of the poems – helped by my bilingual partner, Karin Altenberg. I got to know Monica and Tomas in his last ten years – visiting them in Södermalm and Runmarö. He approved of my English versions, I'm pleased to say, and being on the same stage as him in London, Stockholm and Toronto was a huge honour.

WSM: Violence I would say is a recurring motif in your poetry. Can you explain this?

RR: I'm not sure violence is a *motif* in my work. There is certainly violence in some of the poems, but others deal with desire, awe, grief or dread. I think, increasingly, that the last of these is what I write about most: not violence, but the *fear* of violence. I'm fascinated by that undercurrent of threat – so familiar to those of us who live in big cities: that undertow of barely suppressed anger, the speed and strength and suddenness of dread.

And, anyway, you can't ignore violence. It's in our myths and folk-tales. It's in our lives from the beginning. Any writer has to be sensible to what's around them, and if tension and threat are present and palpable, then they can be subjects. I'm interested in the effects that these anxieties have on people; interested in trying to understand the anxiety – and the violence itself – but mostly I'm interested in the turbulence.

That said, poems are dream-work. They arrive, as I've explained, more often by accident than design. A good example would be a poem of mine called 'At Roane Head', one of a series of invented Scots folk narratives. It feels to me embedded in north-east Scotland through its imagery, language and mythology, and it undeniably contains acts of violence, including the slaughter of physically handicapped children. But I wrote it out in a couple of hours on a still, crisp, sunny afternoon one Christmas in a boathouse on the Norfolk Broads, surrounded by calm water, the occasional splash of bream or perch, and the quacking of ducks.

WSM: Kazuo Ishiguro has written of the rhythm of your 'darkly chiselled poems' and I think that phrase concisely captures the balance between your craft and the fear and dread, and loneliness, that lie behind it. We can conclude by quoting the whole of your poem 'Myth' which I believe captures this feeling in miniature:

> This morning, in bracken
> beyond the east field,
> I find the blown bulbs of sunset;
> on the wet lawn,
> after the snow,
> the snowman's spine.

Once again, thank you, Robin.

John Haynes

Black don't Crack

My wife's skin is as smooth as when we first met
almost thirty years ago, but her eyes have grown
more practical, and when I remind her how
she used to gasp when I touched her, she pretends
she can't remember or talks about shopping or God,
or what happened at work, with the endless petty
racism behind the words and the eyes, unknown
almost to the eyes themselves. Quite a lot about God
because the end-times are coming. And when they do
we'll realise she'd been right. She'll leave a message
on the table here, when she's taken – in rapture –
telling us what we need to do, because she loves us,
prays for us, and wants to see our dear faces
in the next world when we arrive reborn in our bodies,
and she'll be shouting with arms wide wide open –

This morning when I woke up she was sleeping still.
Her leg had come out of the blankets. And had turned silver.

Rachel Mann

Mappa Mundi

This is where cities of salt, brimstone rivers,
faces fixed into the scorched edge of a world
heal into dream.

This is where Cain remembers
the feel of fist on cheekbone, the possibilities
of skin.

This is where vellum recalls lost flesh,
gathers vein, membrane, the frayed fibre of bone
into story,

the maker wanting and not wanting
you to see the mandrakes, the blemmyes
swarming,

no *vade mecum*, but testimony: to god,
his steely throne, his angels made
mere ink,

a triumph *(a judgment?)* etched in beast.

Seán Street

Ghost Variations

*During the night of 17 February, 1854 Robert Schumann wrote a theme 'dictated
by the angels'. While working on variations on this theme he attempted to drown
himself in the Rhine, and was subsequently committed to an asylum. The theme
has been shown to have been previously composed by Schumann himself. It was
his last work.*

A piano holding its breath in the darkness.
A murmur from behind a door, rushing water
on stone, the heard memory of a voice singing
beyond a river obscuring all but the next
room's song. There is no one, no one in the next room,
so a voice is all I have, drowning in distance.

It's the journey inside me makes this a distance
such that now I can barely see through the darkness
towards the door beyond which there's music, a room
and the rushing of the river's noise, its water
moving me note by note on to what happens next,
making memory of a piano's singing.

Variations. Call and response. A voice singing
something new and perfect but heard from a distance
and recalled between one interval and the next,
known silently, as real as all else the darkness
brings through demonic whispers, the rustle water
drowns between me and dictation from the far room.

A piano playing softly in the next room.
Through the held breath of fog in my head there's singing.
I document the moment, music as water
moving downstream, passing, shifting to far distance
as time comes, passes and moves on from one darkness
to another, into whatever happens next.

Note by note, the inevitable in what's next
between where I am and the strange haunted room
that teaches me, the murmuring sound of darkness,
stillness my last chance, the sinking of singing
in the white noise of a river closing distance
across time, hope turned to the music of water.

I now understand the kinship of song and water.
I was on the other side of what happened next
when I began to feel the nearness and distance
of voices pushing together inside my room,
but I never knew it was my own ghost singing,
the ghost of who I once was, somewhere in darkness.

There was the noise of water obscuring the room
before what happened next, the end of all singing,
voices drowned by distance, song blinded by darkness.

Richard Jefferies on the Diving Board

Coate, Wiltshire

By 1935, the Art Deco board at Coate Water provided a nationally renowned platform for diving competitions. It is now listed.

It's an idyll bequeathed to an edge land,
derelict for years, but the ducks love it.
Swindon, if it remembers, Sundays out
here until the dusk makes it depressing.

Time to bed off if you're of the feathered
persuasion, though the M4 never sleeps.
Through years they've learnt to live with that,
far worse is the bearded ghost that troubles

them on full moon nights, him glancing around,
then on impulse executing a perfect
backwards dive, three point five somersaults in
the pike position. Bevis applauding.

Peter McDonald

The Swords

Each out of its embroidered sheath,
flat in the case and bright beneath
two tiny spotlamps at a tilt,
one sword points at another's hilt,
a thin moon against a thin moon
showing clear in the sky at noon,
except this room is dark and there's
no sky, where many swords in pairs
point at each other in the light
which only just fills those airtight
plush spaces inside which they shine
and never move: these two align
themselves, as the occasion serves,
on open and enclosing curves.

They might be parts of a circle which
will never close here, as they pitch
in an arrested sweep of force
that zooms to sever or divorce
one thing from any other thing
it cuts across, that breaks the ring
its own shape is a part of; now
they neither allow nor disallow
the fearful step, the sure defeat,
like two lovers who dare not meet
ever again, so terrible
the strength between them when they pull
into each other's range, or start
to feel themselves drawing apart.

And terrible is not the word:
turn a deaf ear to such absurd
efforts to state the awful thing,
the truth without its clinching ring
which you can almost hear sound out

behind that rough and sudden shout
of anger riven with sheer grief
coming, predictable and brief,
to break in two your every night –
no word for that is ever right,
yet could be caught somewhere between
two pointing blades with their worked sheen;
steel isn't pure, but the pure steel
divides all you can speak and feel.

Outside, the sky is full of flakes
where falling cherry-blossom makes
hanami-clouds above the heads
of picnickers on dry grass beds,
the flasks and paper cups, the neat
parcels of shopping at their feet,
and blows across the paths across
the park, bunches like candy-floss
at each corner, sweet-softening
the hard edges of everything,
to shuffle up in weightless drifts
that even a weak breeze soon lifts,
as crowds move slowly through, and go
in between flower-lights, high and low.

But you are in this room alone:
for minutes now, your eyes have grown
used to the nearly-dark, and so
fixed on the cases' low-power glow
that all they see is pair on pair
of swords contained in dustless air
as if vision were sharp and hard,
tempered, and never off its guard,
cutting straight through the things it sees
with looks like blades, and blades like these;
yet even as it holds its ground
such eyesight turns itself around,
swivelling the held force within
to try an edge against your skin.

Force seems to cancel force, but no:
force locks on force, and they both go
pushing into each other, long
past any stage of being strong;
a stillness ready to explode
from weaknesses that never showed
in centuries, but might be there,
impossible to see or bear –
two swords in a whole room of swords
displayed so that they point towards
each other beneath air and glass
don't move, yet still won't let you pass
now that you want to be away;
older than you, but here to stay.

On the Rocks

Ice in a swivelled glass
coats itself in vermouth;
the colder evenings pass,
and stars over the roof
back away to a mild
dome in the distance, as
each one is ranged and filed
by quadrant, azimuth.

The ice-cubes snick and clunk:
behind us, a cliff face;
ahead, pale and part-sunk
in shadow, the last trace
of daytime on broad streets
recedes, where traffic's race
is a bright line that repeats
itself to bound this place.

If stars figure the truth,
it's one that we can't read;
in between lip and tooth,
ice numbs whatever need
there is to make my mouth
say what has to be said
long past the end of youth:
a good or a bad deed.

The Table

An empty plate of stone
cools nothing more than air,
its purpose only one
damaged beyond repair,
as cells by the million
invisibly expire,
not to be back again
exactly as they were.

Nobody comes to say
what to be ready for;
what good it does to play
brave, and to shut the door
thinking we have the way
to make its hinges stir;
hearts we broke in a day
broken for evermore.

What was done on the spur
proves to be done for good,
and I cannot prepare
a shadowy ghost food,
spreading leaves everywhere
and scattering out crude
mosses like scraps of fur
over blunt shreds of wood.

Danielle Hope

Rock

I speak to you but nothing
not a flinch
you grey assembly of stone
you pile of nothings

you slate coloured
collection
tumbling to hissing
spitting surf

to which you also
say nothing.
The sea might rage
but you are deaf

sunlight falls over you
bathers climb and
lie on you but you
are unmoved. Even

if I rub my hands red
on your scaly face
there is nothing.
And when night falls

you seem to lean
into the gale
so that nothing
can find shelter.

Ruth O'Callaghan

Survivor

and the sins of the fathers

Then, the trains were not the worst of the matter.
Now I know that so many arrived meant so many had died.

Father said it was a season of renewal, like corn.
I was to obey him at all times. He would protect me.

I asked if he meant the thick smoke that harmed lungs
He kissed me. Called me *Son*. Said nothing of the ash.

The ash would creep in. I was forbidden to open my window.
Forbidden to play outside. That was the worst of the matter.

I would hear the others outside. They were silent,
marching barefoot on stones. I sang to the tune of the gravel.

I envied their game of picking leaves, swallowing them
before their guide turned. Like *What's the time, Mr. Wolf?*

When the trees were leafless and the grass gone,
they dug in the mud. Father said there's nutrients in mud.

I knew they liked me – they gave Father toys they'd made.
A top from bone or a doll so real its hair and skin felt like mine.

I didn't thank them. Father said he'd make sure they knew
how matters stood. I never saw them again.

I was forbidden to look out but I heard their high, strange song.
That was the day everyone was running.

The smoke was thicker. The ash covered the house, entered it.
Father shouted at me.

He pulled papers, dashed outside with great bundles.
The sun glinted on his buttons. Others rushed past, didn't salute.

Some soldiers scrabbled at the gate. Father had to discipline them.
The gate stayed shut. The soldiers motionless, playing *Fish*.

Mother threw clothes in a case. Father travelled in civilian clothes.
In Nuremberg I heard a sparrow. I think I was six.

Faye Joy

Take it out

Take the old bed out, take out
the state of the sleep-easy, love-ease:
gone.
He slept in it, sexed in it and died in it.
I lie on his side of the bed, facing the wall
where the fireplace was, now blocked off.
I cannot toss or turn, just stare.
Take the old bed out,
take it out, tear the fabric, watch
yellowed mattress lumps
tumble from ragged lips.
One cantilevered drawer skews
over the kiltered frame, spied through
the rime-frosted window of its
waiting room, the empty house next door.
Coffee-slicks, love-stains, scorch-scrolls,
palimpsests crudely exposed, years of bed-lies
come to this – take the old bed out.

Sheenagh Pugh

Wher beth they, bifore us weren?

For it is impossible for anything to come to be from what is not, and it cannot be brought about that that which is should be utterly destroyed.

Empedocles

Seeded in the dark, it hankered for sky:
it shouldered beyond the forest shade
to touch sunlight. Under an axe
it became a house, a boat, a book,
lived a new life, fell from use
to kindling: the fire caught and blew it
to flinders that flew and cooled to ash.
Or it crashed and rotted, eaten with age,
into earth, under it, stifled, pressed
beneath lifetimes, ice ages, until it hardened
into diamond or anthracite.

And the poet who riddled it took a pen
from a greylag's wing that had flown oceans.
He made ink of oak-galls, rust, rainwater
and he laid his words on a calf's skin
that ended its days as a kitchen rag.
Then he fell, he too, back to earth,
leaving his song in the ears of many,
hoping that they, before the air
forgot their voices, would throw it on,
like a ball that passes from hand to hand,
never falling.
                    Should it console us somehow
that what looks so like annihilation
is only change? That beaches were cliffs,
that coal was once leaf, that flesh and bone,
even, become humus and lime
to feed new life? If this is comfort,
why does our breath catch, our heart turn over
when a dead man is lifted from permafrost
or peat bog with his face still on,

55

looking as if you could shake his shoulder
and wake him?
                        We've no cause to love change,
that's the truth of it. Surely something
is lost; surely a body is
not just limbs, but their running lightness,
not eyes only, but what lit them,
and where does that go, Empedocles,
what becomes of it?
                        The ball passes
from hand to hand, but its colours
fade in the sun: one day, perhaps,
it drops in the grass, lies half hidden,
its purple weathered to grey.

And it may be a poem, so perfect
it lives on the page or tongue
for long ages of men,
but it may be no more
than a neighbour's good nature,
a workman's craft, a joker's quick wit,
and these are soon gone, as soon
as the last man dies
who kept them in mind,
yet they *were*, as surely as cliff and leaf,
but where is the sand, the coal
that came of them?

Is there a beach somewhere,
unmapped, unvisited, whose sand
was ground from the soft stone
of all that has slipped from mind?
Could we run through our hands
the grains of a girl's longing,
an artist's gift, a palaeolithic jest?

Show me the sand, Empedocles,
show me the sand.

Terence Dooley

Multiverse

Winter now, the window stays closed tight.
Imperfect aperture, all it admits
is light. As if on oath it cannot help
dispensing information like a mouth.

But it has several lights and several ways
to modify the things it says, the things
it can't take back. It lets in different days:
one annelidan, wriggling like a cage
of serpentine, one salt-encrusted,
like a shawl of greys, and one a clear gaze.

So which is the true light? Because the pane
is flawed, because glass travels and descends,
or buckles like a skeleton with age,
is what it utters blurred and fanciful,
how many tears have dried to hide a truth,
unhindered light is distant from its source.
Open the window then, let time decide.

David Hale

Accordion Crime

It sat proud in the police auction,
amidst the stuffed parrots,
suit-cases, carpets and whisks,

a real piece of craftsmanship
with its inlay, fretwork
and bakelite strips.

Lifted from the premises
of some ageing tunesmith
who'd failed to drop the latch

on his way back from the Duke,
it ended up in the monthly sale:
scuffed, a little worse for wear,

a couple of keys gapped
like old teeth, but wheezing still,
dreaming of foxtrot and tango,

a pearl amongst swine;
even though I'd never played one,
thirty quid, and it was mine.

David Cooke

Franz Marc, *Der Turm der blauen Pferde*

for Patricia McCarthy

With so much implied in gleaming haunches
– their strength and movement, the sprung weight
of muscles – your eye forgets their flatness:
the image of an image abstracted
from a canvas lost and maybe destroyed.

A fine string of horses making their way
on tentative hooves, they descend the imagined
slope they mirror, reined in by contours.

Aloof or merely bemused, their gaze
roams a garish skyline as far
as the neck's resistance allows,
seeing through and then beyond us
to where our own visions began
in a smoke-filled, flickering cave.

Lances. Sabres. Muskets. Somehow
they have galloped beyond them all
past explosions and mud-clogged wire.

When our noise subsides
and we have vanished, their acolytes
and masters, they will test the air again,
sensing only hushed syllables –
fetlock, withers, stirrup, girth…

Stuart Pickford

The Green Wallpaper

(Edvard Munch called his paintings his children. If they proved difficult, he'd place them around his house.)

Some places were obvious: that sonnet
only fit for spares, dumped in
the odds-and-ends drawer.

The elegy about granddad's pond,
discovering a hoard of newts
in shiny strokes of green,

pinned up in the concrete yard.
A villanelle about my fondness
for the hard stuff, chucked in the recycling.

One stubborn failure had it coming
on the bottom stair while couplets on love
went cold turkey in the garage.

An old one about the ocean in Oz
with lashings of sun, screwed up
in a dying hanging basket

for irony. But what of
my son's anorexia over the years,
paint dribbled and scratched?

I hid the image in the loft.
The ladder creaked in the night.
His face at the end of the bed.

My depression? A self-portrait
on a time-delay, me lunging
in the foreground towards my wife.

I locked it under the stairs
but it's reworked itself to hang
in every room. Like a naughty boy,

I led it by the hand to the skylight
to see for itself that clouds
were new, sun-fringed palettes

but there it is sitting in the respectable
black chair of my father
as heavy, green walls throb.

Gulgurn Manja

The 4x4 is beached
beside the sandy track.
White eucalypts, bark
dangling in strips.

I scrabble up a knoll,
through starry thryptomene
to the Cave of Hands,
the alcoves of Gulgurn Manja.

The hands, the hands greet me.
Twenty six right hands,
children's hands that slotted
into their fathers'.

Stencilled in a southerly wind
while baking possums,
upon returning each year
or, who knows, for fun.

Lines record visitors
as long as 20,000 years ago
and emu tracks when Canopus
drifts into the Milky Way.

Despite the grille, the shelter's
full of northern sun
and shaped to my back –
and the hands, the hands

applaud around the walls.
In my mind, I add
one line to the rest
and place my palm on theirs.

Note:

Gulgurn Manja means 'children's hands' in Jardwadjali; it is situated in the
Grampians, Victoria.

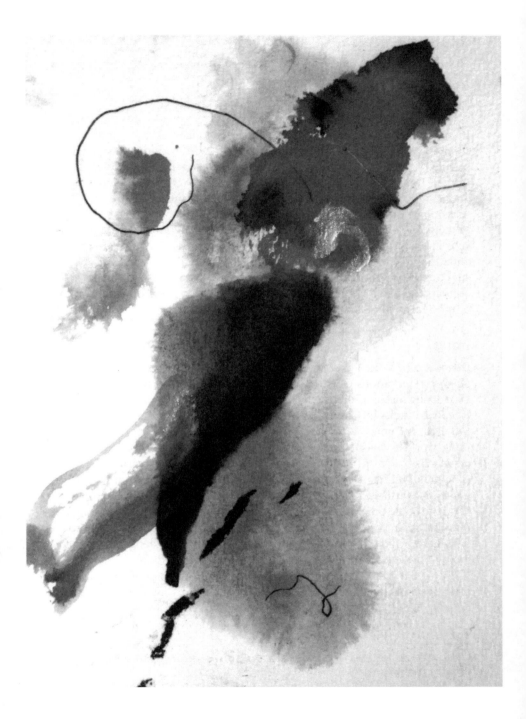

Martin Caseley

Rain Falling in the Far West:
some themes in the recent poetry of John F Deane

In musical terms, a semibreve is defined as the longest note in common use; John F Deane's latest collection *Semibreve*[1] swiftly follows his generous selected poems, *Snow Falling on Chestnut Hill*, and in many ways, is a step further. Deane has been quite prolific in recent years, and this most recent publication is impressively lauded by Rowan Williams as demonstrating a 'passionate and searching engagement' with the local and physical God... of the gospels'. This recommendation succeeds in highlighting some of the substantial religious elements in Deane's recent poetry, but his work is more wide-ranging, textured and carefully-woven than this rather austere phrase suggests. My aim in this essay is to explore some of the common notes regularly sounded within his recent poetry, including, aptly, his regular use of musical symbolism.

Hares

Deane's 2008 volume, *A Little Book of Hours,* featured several long religious poems, explorations of Old Testament events, particularly those featuring David, and also conscious evocations of psalms and religious iconography. It feels a little coldly monastic at times, from the title onwards: a poem like 'Towards a Conversion' offers a bleak picture of God's historical presence – the world is 'indifferent' and a crow, 'a monkish body hooded/ in grey crawks its blacksod, cleansing music'[2]. Deane was to find warmer creatures as symbols in his succeeding volumes, and also a return to the power of music. Nevertheless, it is a slight relief when, in one of the final poems, 'Triduum', the poet moves away from his devotional reading of Dante, out into the fresh air and a Saturday full of hares playing in the meadows. A baby hare, which first seems dead, slowly lopes off, insolently alive: many more of these creatures were to appear in succeeding volumes.

Eye of the Hare, Deane's 2011 book, seems a more confident, warmer offering altogether. In the title poem, the poet turns away from shooting an easy target, 'perplexed', but aware of the 'green world/ easy under

---

[1] Both collections published by Carcanet, in 2015 and 2012 respectively. Rowan Williams' quote taken from the back cover of *Semibreve*.

[2] All quotations from Deane's poems are from the volumes discussed in the main body of the text.

sunlight', he intuits in the hare's eye. This green world features more and more strongly in many more recent poems, and he feels duly blessed and absolved of his actions: in 'The Hare', the creature appears again, 'white belly-bib and scut, the ears/ like tablespoons filled up with snow'. In a third poem, 'Dusk', the hare reappears, a 'big-limbed loper, who sat, quietened now, priest-like on our grass', living 'in a certain low-mass, sacramental intensity'. Shape-shifters, tricksters, familiars and symbols, hares have a long and honourable history in poetry; William Cowper famously wrote of keeping them as pets. In myth, they are connected with the inconstancy of the moon: hares will 'appear suddenly in an unexpected place; stand up or leap precipitately... pause a moment, dart off at speed, only to reappear a few moments later running in an entirely different direction.'[3]

This natural world is no longer a monastic, levelling presence, recalling perhaps the stony, doubtful landscapes of R S Thomas, but instead new tones of sacramental wonder and green mysticism begin to emerge. 'This is where I would push the poem to go', Deane writes in 'Birds, Beasts and Buttercups', 'deeper still, where all that is living touches roots...of earth's exposed harmonies'. 'Harmonies' is a word used over and over again in Deane's poetry and this hidden music of pattern and wonder is evident, too, in the poems of childhood in the Achill Islands: in 'Between Worlds', he describes 'harmonies sensed among furze blossoms/ and the assonant humming of the bees'. This wonder also seeks to transcend in several poems: in 'Roots', for example, Deane describes 'raindance on the motorways' and 'grace-filled sycamores...among the every-morning miracles.'

In this volume we do not hear the stern tones of the Old Testament kings: instead, in 'Lives of the Minor Poets', he lists the names of prophets who

> fling their hands up in their rage before they pass
> into the ringing silence of the Good Book; all you hear
> is a contented humming, like bumble-bees...

They, too, are now heard as part of the symphonic pattern of the natural world.

Ghosts

Growing up on Achill Island has always given Deane a rich fund of memory and beauty to recreate whilst growing deeper as a writer. It also informs his sense of spiritual apartness. The sequence 'Achill; The Island' allows

---

[3] Quoted from *The Leaping Hare* by George Ewart Evans and David Thomson (Faber, 1972, p. 113), a fascinating study of all aspects of the hare, particularly in mythology and folklore.

him space to explore this Edenic place, 'isle of sparrows' ('Inishgalloon') where a ruined monastery is silent but 'attending till the Spirit comes again' ('The Monastery'). Here, Deane describes himself as one who came to light a candle, 'a small flame, like a word that would/ hold within itself the tidal pull of our beloved dead', and his poems celebrating growing up there are full of word-pictures struggling to contain the thronging ghostly presences and memories.

'Who Have Gone Before', from *Eye of the Hare,* also describes the 'ragged, glad processions' of insubstantial presences, joyful in their freedom; this poem, too, compares the 'saints and martyrs' who are the subject of prayer to humbler evidence of renewal – primroses, daffodils, 'gangs of long-tailed jittery tits' – which paradoxically leaves the poet lost for words and convinced of his own arrogance.

'Shelf Life', also in this collection, is tuned to a humbler key: the poet lovingly itemises the contents of kitchen shelves before ending with 'me, here/ mooching about in my ghosthood over shelves no longer there.' The vivid pictures of the various items redolent of the past – almanacs, tins, Lego bricks – convince the reader of the presence of such things, then comes the admission that they are now all gone. The poet is the only ghostly presence, just as in 'November', from *Semibreve*, where 'the beloved dead' are glimpsed sociably filling a parlour, talking and laughing, he is the only observer: 'I/ stand distraught outside the great blurred window/ looking in'. The dead, joking, bustling about, are figures akin to those resurrected in the paintings of Stanley Spencer. Like Spencer, too, Deane includes the numinous pull of the quotidian and everyday. 'Still Life', from the latest volume, uses the device of a painting to lead into a list-poem, returning to 'the scullery of the old yellow house', but here Deane concludes differently: these humble domestic items are 'all solid things/ redeeming us though we stand silent, helpless, and in hope'. There is a redemptive value to these word-pictures and the childhood they conjure up.

The other ghostly presence in the childhood parlour for any Irish writer creating such pictures is, of course, Seamus Heaney. In this respect, Deane's Achill is not far distant from Heaney's Dublin, and poems such as 'In the Margins' and 'Butcher', both from *Semibreve*, are heavily indebted to early Heaney poems, especially the ur-poem for all aspirant Irish poets seeking to depict their calling, 'Digging'.[4] Heaney's pen is a powerful tool, marking the distance between himself and his father, whereas Deane pictures the local scholar's 'plump and easy-tempered/ fountain pen' ushering him in

---

4 'Digging', from *Death of a Naturalist,* Seamus Heaney (Faber, 1966); 'Butcher' could profitably be read alongside 'A Constable Calls' from *North* (Faber, 1975).

to the priestly 'steady/ application to the word' and the mysteries of the writer's craft.

Having said this, several of the brief pictures collected in *Snow Falling on Chestnut Hill* display a lyrical grace all Deane's own: 'Sheets', for instance, with its beautiful picture of washing-day is another Stanley Spencer view, airy and light. Elsewhere, there are the 'ghosts of your loved dead ...drifting by, offshore' in 'Midsummer Poem', but there is 'no need to fear' them as they 'hold within them...their own light' and will 'resurface, firmer in themselves, and more fruitful', a consolatory picture of a new season of growth and resurrection. Heaney's landscape, even in comparatively minor early poems such as 'Storm on the Island'[5], is keyed to a more violent, tragic force, the fear of a 'huge nothing'; Deane's most ethereal landscapes are, by contrast, thronged and populated, even if only by the dead contained in his words.

Notes

The binding force in all Deane's landscapes is musical: a symphonic 'long struggle/ towards the harmonies', as 'Unfinished Symphony' in *Semibreve* puts it. This poem, ending a sequence mourning his brother, gives us hares, jackdaws, owls and all the booming history of Ireland as a 'part-notated manuscript', but the healing, ordering power of music has been a long-standing feature of his verse.

'Between Worlds'[6] goes back to Deane's origins, his schooldays 'in a two-roomed school' where this is first sensed, in insect sounds and classroom chants where the poet recognises 'the first echoes of a music, certain in its structuring, grounded, pure, a deep... prelude'. Capturing this is a life-long quest, however, while beyond the practising of scales 'the symphony of that wild world plays on' ('Well-Tempered Clavier') and devoted practice can lead only to 'cacophonies' and 'confusions'. Deane's view of the allure of this leads him to view music as a spiritual organisation of the world in 'More':

> It approaches the heaving of the sea, even, at times,
> the crashing of waves against the coast
> in dark-day Atlantic storms. More than the lilt
>
> of a Brandenburg concerto...

Even when all of it is recognised for what it is, there is no mastering of it: 'Then more', the poem concludes.

---

[5] In *Death of a Naturalist*.
[6] These three poems are all from *Eye of the Hare*.

'Writing out the Myth', from *Snow Falling on Chestnut Hill*, explores this lifelong calling, using the figure of Anton Brückner to set the potency of music against poets (notably the metaphysicals) and the journey Deane has taken from Achill. Brückner, priestly, is pictured assembling harmonies whilst Deane travels to Sofia and considers the way that he has come. Struggles with literacy, words and the demands of the first person open up access to a chain of linked ideas:

> ...soon it would be joined-up
> writing; I would be part of it, a link in the Altamira chain
>
> through Achill Island
> to Zimbabwe. The word. The Word. Traveller...

From A to Z, these 'linked signs' offer order, but one word, the first person singular, remains problematic: 'I have never got it right', Deane admits.

The next section of this poem offers a list of poetic and musical harmonists: Donne, Herbert, Elgar, Brahms – but despite the 'nubs/ of spirit-wings', a suitably metaphysical conceit, Deane admits he is 'relearning ignorance' in order to write with the freedom of foolishness, and aspire to a chain of witnesses taken from scripture (Paul) and myth (Icarus). Icarus is 'in preparation for the myth', whilst Deane can only write it out, laboriously, as if back in the schoolroom, learning his letters: Bruckner, meanwhile, is glimpsed again, accepting that his Ninth Symphony will be unfinished, laughing. 'Pastoral Symphony', which follows this sequence, gives us another musical icon, Handel, who sought to offer 'heart-warming clarities' to the poor. For Deane, once again, 'the faithful ones' are a ghostly throng, but 'the usefulness of poetry' when placed alongside 'the tasking poetry of the spirit' is questioned. The letters can never be learnt, the word is never fully mastered, the musical notes never fully set down.

In his latest collection, four poems in particular return to this theme, although there are many other musical references in the fabric of others. The title poem, 'Semibreve', returns to childhood on Achill once again: the young Deane in a chapel, 'entranced/ by sacrament', becomes aware of an inner vibration, 'the first semibreve sounded of a gifted music'. 'Tuned for it', he listens and waits. The playing of Bach, in 'Viola D'Amour' offers a simple account of such an epiphany: walls dissolve and the musician is lifted into eternity, the soul 'ringing with immortality' between the notes played. Harmonies, both spiritual and musical, are suddenly revealed between the dizzying echoes.

In terms of form, Deane has returned to smaller, self-contained, regular stanzas in contrast to the long, complex, interconnected sequences found in the earlier volumes. 'Playing on the White Notes' makes a virtue of this relative simplicity. The natural, pastoral world is again evident in butterflies, lambs and Michaelmas daisies, all linked by colour. This is a visual harmony, the only musical reference being in the title, where the black notes of the night are implied by the powerful contrasting white 'splintering of stars' and the 'fullness of the moon'. 'Tuning' finds the poet listening, inspired by someone else playing 'Bach, Buxtehude, Peters' and that listening attitude is a willing waiting, listening to the rhythms of time passing in the countryside, 'April/ whispering over into May'. These are 'approximations to a symphony', ordinary days which become tense with searching, with expectation: the poet tuning himself, as Donne once wrote: 'I shall be made thy Musique; as I come/ I tune the instrument here at the dore'.[7]

Following on from a sequence on the death of his brother, Deane approaches this idea in 'Unfinished Symphony': back in Ireland, aware of the 'cacophonous' history of the place, he notices that 'all the earth is rife again/ with the part-notated manuscript of a symphony.' This impossibly complex tapestry, 'the long struggle/ towards the harmonies' is finally validated by anticipation of 'that great finale…that thunderous Amen!' The incarnation, the word, in all its Pauline complexity, will be spoken; in the meantime, there are 'the false notes./ the wrong keys' struck.

The Far West

The title of this essay comes from one of the poems in *Semibreve*: Deane returns, 'old and self-absorbed as Lear', to his kingdom, the bogland of the far west. He wonders where he has been, and why; he turns away to what is left; as an achievement, poetry feels 'like turf-dust'. He considers the dangerous myths of such a landscape; but then is cheered by 'epiphany/ in the movement of a fox.' Below the 'wallow-surface of belief', he senses a heartbeat; out there, forgiveness can be sought; bells ring; he waits, aware of the endless, falling rain. In the final, famous, lilting paragraph of James Joyce's 'The Dead'[8], Gabriel Conroy, standing by the window watching the snow fall, wonders if it is time to begin on his journey west. He becomes aware of the presence of the dead and his solid world begins to dissolve. For Deane, 'rain is falling…as it has ever fallen', but candles light the windows and beyond the word, he turns to what is left – the spirit.

---

[7] 'Hymne to God, my God, in my sicknesse', John Donne, *The Divine Poems*, edited by Helen Gardner, Oxford University Press, 1952.
[8] From *Dubliners*, originally published in 1914.

John F Deane

Epithalamium

for Mary and Nicholas

I see you, stilled, attentive, in arrivals hall, love, yet tentative,
somewhere in the air;
I wished, back then, when the white beauty of the frosted earth
was powering the crocus, hyacinth, and daffodil,

that the most perfect snowflakes fall like kisses on your cheeks;
I prayed that –
to the questions you would need to ask – the answers might always be
the loveliness and wonder

of creation. Hold, then, to astonishment, to the ongoing mystery
of one another, the burgeoning familiar;
we have come to understand that when the singing ends
the song continues,

when the poem is written at last, the poetry begins, we have learned
that patience is difficult at the threshold
and in the forecourt of the heart. Be aware of the possibility of grief
and of the conceivable presence of the angel.

I see you, stilled, attentive, at the altar steps,
the bright loveliness of beginnings like a veil about you,
the hearts and prayers of a community
behind you, and this we pray to the God of sacrament:

that she may grace you both to be
magnificent together, magnificent to one another, magnificent
through the bountiful flight ahead.
We wish you music, the slow, classical dance

of what is past and yet to come, the heady beat
of the fleeting present; we wish you sunlight, the reach and sounding
of the waters about Keem Bay,
the gentle breathing of the Atlantic; that all weathers be a force about you,

keeping you faithful to the fluency of symphony.
I see you, stilled, attentive, in the bright dawn, love urging the grace
of a sure journey upon you, your destination
a better world, of love and mercy, of justice, happiness and peace.

All Shall be Well

for Laura, on her birthday, April 2015

How comes it I have been reasoned down to thinking
that miracle is not so? Not really wine, then, save
in the minds of those blessed at the feast; no actual storm
was swamping the boat where the Christ slept before he rose

to rebuke the winds and the waters; he whose word
or touch might release a soul from torment. I cannot doubt
the everyday wonders through which I move, for the mere
commonplace is life and life is miracle. And love.

Firefly and anaconda. Pollen, seed, and catkin. Gravity
and uplift. Poems gifted and the soft inducements
of music. How bread was broken, blessed and shared
in a hostelry at Emmaus. And so the morning candle

is plea and offering, faith's seduction, that we may keep
a wise heart and live in perfect peace amongst impossibles.

Omar Sabbagh

Only Plenitude at The Void:
The Sacred Music in Christian Wiman's *every riven thing*

> To love is to feel your death
> given to you like a sentence,
> to meet the judge's eyes
> as if there were a judge,
> as if he had eyes,
> and love.
>
> 'Gone For The Day, She Is The Day'

Christian Wiman's spiritual meditation, *My Bright Abyss,* is in my view on a par with another outstanding spiritual autobiography from just over a century earlier, *Orthodoxy* by G.K. Chesterton. Indeed, in the 'Preface' of perhaps the most penetrating book written about Chesterton, Hugh Kenner's *Paradox in Chesterton,* Marshall McLuhan avers that Chesterton possessed a 'metaphysical intuition of being.' And I'd say the same about Wiman. Part of the 'metaphysical' aspect of Wiman's gambits in this superlative collection, *every riven thing*, shows up in how integrated the formal craftsmanship is with the sentiments expressed thereby. Wiman is both like Eliot's 'metaphysical poets' in this sense, anything but dissociated, as well as in a very pronounced way echoic of Eliot himself.

The first poem in the collection, 'Dust Devil,' starts us in Wiman's childhood, 'in a time when time stopped.' The devilishness of the toy 'top' detailed in the poem is a complement to the toying of both child and adult author, recollecting – but more than this, as we'll see, the devilry of Fate or God toying with him. In this thin-versed poem, Wiman speaks of his 'art' in paradoxes, as 'flourishing / vanishing,' or as artifact of both, 'cohesion / illusion.' And this tallies with his (already mentioned) superbly poised spiritual meditation, where he follows in the footsteps of the likes of Bonhoeffer and Weil, and the Jurgen Moltmann of *The Crucified God.* Whether we call it 'affliction,' 'the void,' or what have you, these Christian thinkers were eminently modernist in seeing God, not as necessity, but as 'contingency.' The essence of Christ's mission resided for them in his penultimate words, about having been 'forsaken.' These thinkers – Wiman in their train – locate God, plenitude or infinity, precisely in His absconding and voiding. God is the god of reality, thus: which means that the essence of mortal life is what happens to you, shorn of your own egotistical intentionality or wishes or projections. If God is the Real, then there's nothing romantic about God.

The next feature that struck me about this collection was how often Wiman thematized poetry itself. By this I don't mean the idea expressed in 'This Mind Of Dying,' in which the prayer runs, 'My God my grief forgive my grief tamed in language / to a fear that I can bear;' or, later, in 'Late Fragment' the implicit redemption of a painful memory by way of sweet musicality:

> My father was a boatbuilder.
> Prow of a man, his world a sea to cleave.
> I learned a dangerous patience,
> to navigate night, live on nothing, leave.

What I mean is that poetry in essence is the alienation of selfhood into language; in this sense, poetry finds its apogee in the lack of self-regard, which latter tends towards unwitting self-occlusion. We see this effective 'othering,' for instance, in the arced use of a 'tree,' 'the unyielding one,' in 'After The Diagnosis,' or, later, in the telling list:

> All stories stop: once more you're lost
> in something I can merely see:
> steam spiriting out of black coffee,
> the scorched pores of toast, a bowl
> of apple butter like edible soil...

Or then, opening the closing poem of the first section, 'A Good Landscape For Grief:'

> A good landscape for grief
> has no hill higher than a furrow,
> a few gouty cacti,
> perhaps a withered tree or two
> if only to remind you
> of what's missing.

For all his speculative boldness, Wiman's descriptive flair evinces both a highly refined (and playful) ear and a truly seeing eye: both, immanently. Highly idiosyncratic, effortlessly fresh, as well as deeply accessible and engaging, we read of how – speaking of an adult neighbour from his childhood – he 'loved the eyesore opulence / of his five partial cars, the wonder-cluttered porch / with its oilspill plumage...' ('Five Houses Down').

Homonyms and puns loom large in the collection. In 'The Mole' we open with 'After love / discovers it....' Which is to say, something age-old: 'discovering.' And then, embracing both 'moles' – cancerous blemish and animal-metaphor – we read how 'he breaks

> into a wide
> smile, as if joy
> were the animal
> in him, blind,
> scrabbling, earth-
> covered creature
> tunneling
> up from God...

Paradox and punning again, here towards the end of the second installment of 'Not Altogether Alone:'

> When there is nothing left to curse
> you can curse nothing
> but when there is nothing left to love
> the heart eats inward and inward its own need
> for release...

Nuanced laughter in the face of tragedy, again, in the fifth installment of the latter:

> To live amid the jackal looks of unlove,
> all the relatives circling eerily warily the scent
> of their own blood...

And in 'Voice Of One Head,' a poem which tells tales from 9/11, we read of how, 'It seemed there was not one of us / not one of us....'

There are echoes of other devotional poets throughout the collection. Donne's sonnet, praying to a 'three-personed-God,' is evoked when we read at the end of 'Small Prayer In A Hard Wind,' 'shatter me God into my thousand sounds.' By turns, Wiman is synaesthetic, as when in 'And I Said To My Soul, Be Loud,' he speaks (somewhat mock-heroically) of how 'the sound the sun would make / if the sun could make a sound.' Re-visiting the theme of constituting the sacred from radical contingency, perhaps there's something of Eliot's 'etherized' patient closing the following (later in the last-mentioned poem):

> For I am come a whirlwind of wasted things
> and I will ride this tantrum back to God
>
> until my fixed self, my fluorescent self
> my grief-nibbling, unbewildered, wall-to-wall self
> withers in me like a salted slug.

The eponymous poem, 'every riven thing,' uses difference in repetition across a highly taut, but nonetheless effortlessly fluent form. Wiman thematizes how existence ('thing') is only itself or only becomes itself as 'riven.' 'To believe is to believe you have been torn / from the abyss, yet stand waveringly on its rim,' ('One Time'); '...I say God and mean more / than the bright abyss that opens in that word,' (from the second installment of the same).

Singing in 'I Sing Insomnia,' we read at the last of how the poet is:

> awake
>   my little while
> alive
>   without a why

The chiselling of his craft away from maudlin elegy marks, in my view, the authority of Wiman's spiritual endeavours. This soulful maturity is articulated in the penultimate stanza of the collection's eponymous poem:

> God goes belonging to every riven thing. He's made
> the things that bring him near,
> made the mind that makes him go.
> A part of what man knows,
> apart from what man knows...

That final instance of word-play sums it up: the fertile antinomy of a god abandoned by god; a god – thus abandoned – who can therefore be God, for us, riven as we are, inside our mortal coil, by privation, natural and moral.

Christian Wiman

If I Could Write a Cry

If I could write a cry
if I could reduce

or maybe raise
all music to a moan

savage unsayable psalm
barb and balm

of my unbreakable heart

Assembly

It may be Lord our voice is suited now
only for irony, onslaught, and the minor hierarchies of rage.

It may be that only the crudest, cruelest transformations touch us,
gauzewalkers in the hallways of a burn ward.

I remember a blind man miraculous for the sounds of his mouth,
every bird rehearsed and released for the children to cheer.

Where is he now, in what icy facility or sunlit square,
blackout shades and a brambled mouth, singing extinctions?

Maitreyabandhu

Reading Cavafy

You wish you could remember an August evening
when you were twenty-one or twenty-five,
a rented room where you could hear the sea
and where the moon shone weakly through thin
and partially-opened curtains near an old taverna
or by a railway track, the hot night hushed
or noisy with tables being cleared away, revellers,
a motorino starting somewhere in an alley;
or perhaps up in an attic room above a tobacconist
at the top of a creaking stair with him asleep
on gull-white, sex-entangled sheets like a boy
from Antioch or Samothrace, his hair awry,
your love a glass set down and drained,
waiting for morning to fill it full again.

The World of Senses

I yearn for this much-prized, painful love –
his smile, the way he moves his hips
when he cuts a loaf or stirs a soup
or my chest against his back – this love
that quietly lifts away when he falls asleep.

I yearn for this much-desired success –
vaulting ambition, rapt applause
as I bend to take my seat, awards
received in feigned surprise – success
that barely adds a farthing to my store.

But I never yearn for you, the Lotus Born –
frown and smile and trident staff,
illumined image through which I'd pass
beyond this world of senses, borne
across the waters, safely, by your raft.

Antony Mair

The Stopped Clocks

i.m. Daniel de Calf

Time's wingèd chariot speeds, but sometimes stands
quite still. You shambled in one afternoon,
spitting English through Dutch consonants.
With hands that seemed too large for tiny cogs
you lifted our French clock from a cardboard box,
restored to its Second Empire elegance.
Two other clocks now wait for you in vain,
their movements stopped. On one, as if in grief,
a seated maiden lowers her gilded lyre;
on the other, Cupid stoops, resting his bow
on an alabaster plinth. Where you are now,
the skill of measuring the passing hour
is obsolete. An idle afterlife
seems alien to those industrious hands.

Colin Wilcockson

Sagittarius: Archer of the Year's End

Soft shadows shade my garden from the flame
Of last leaves flickering on the chestnut boughs:
I fear the winter archer's ice-shaft aim.

Past is my age of dreams which have no name
Too late fulfilling promises and vows:
Soft shadows shade my garden from the flame.

Now quiet acceptance without praise or blame
Ambition lost that its brief fame endows:
I fear the winter archer's ice-shaft aim.

So let this garden to the world proclaim
That past and future shall not grief espouse:
Soft shadows shade my garden from the flame.

Conkers bright-gleaming in a childhood game
Conjure up spirits, memories arouse:
I fear the winter archer's ice-shaft aim.

Defiant verses strive yet to declaim
Dream-visions caught in moments while I drowse:
Soft shadows shade my garden from the flame –
I fear the winter archer's ice-shaft aim.

Carole Bromley

Just Friends

'Friendship may, and often does, grow into love
but love never subsides into friendship'.
                              Byron

Yet it's your friendship I miss the most,
the way we were so easy with each other,
the way your body would turn to mine
and smiling was like looking in the mirror.

Afterwards my face would ache
with all those muscles
that hadn't had a work out in months.
Now I feel them wasting again.

So much more than friends
and now so much less. As if someone
had pulled a plug out of the wall
and the world had gone dark.

This morning at the arboretum

I hoped to find you there. We do that, don't we?
Go back to places to keen over stones or trees
or, in my case, a little jar of wild flowers,
one of the ones Alastair put on the tables.
You'd have approved. Just daisies and grass.
While no-one was looking I stroked the petals
as if I was touching your face. Just that.
In the background, coffee machine, clatter of cups,
a dog drinking from a bowl as if he was dying of thirst.

Afterwards I walked up the long mown drives
and the grasses either side whispered,
here and there among them a poppy, a geranium,
a purple orchid. It's the month of purple, isn't it?
If you were here you could tell me why. In the wood
a mass of purple foxgloves, growing wild.
I sat on a bench and closed my eyes.
Just a distant plane, a bird's chira chira cheee,
bees visiting each mauve flower, the hush of trees.

Merryn Mac Carthy

Like the Swallow

You dart here and there
like the swallow, glissando.
When do you return –
is the distance too great?
Quand est-ce-que tu reviendras?

You take off like a word
about to be expressed,
a wish nearly fulfilled,
denying all constraints.
What passions do you seek?

The headlights of a car dip, flash
on the hill rushing home,
wherever home is. The road
twists and turns
in my heart.

Acacias are heady with flower.
If I could only stay you
long enough to embrace,
gently I would release you
into infinite space.

Reiki

I listen to the water ripple
powered by a presence,
the reverberating language
of his strokes.

Visit upon visit
the uncertain hazard.
Hands that know me
skin and bone.

Heat that breaches
boundaries, finds auras, stars
which hold strange light.
In French or English

how can I express
the reaches? Healing oils
slowly drip, and then
these sudden singing rivulets.

Roger Elkin

North Ferriby Foreshore, remembering

i.m. Granddad Charles and Peter Reading who never met

Not sand, but reaches of mudflat
veined by rainbowy seawater-seeps
along the Humberside strand. And,
further out, a pewter gleam where
the Trent – water within water –
fattens to estuary's broad blade, then
wider still, circle-swirls to mouth
at silent horizons, the North Sea,
Europe and beyond.

Seems worlds away from Trent's
well-head and its insignificant sibilants
trickling through Bailey's farmyard.

How memories tumble. To hills.
And home: the moorland village
cricked safe in England's vertebrae
where gritstone walling collects
the fields' purposes.

And to Granddad – simple man
crowned local bigwig – mouthing down
his home-grown workmates,
*Thait senatucked.**

Laugh at that. That bastardised Latin
he hadn't even had chance to learn
let alone forget, any more than he'd
heard of Ferriby. Or estuary.
Though knew belonging,
like the sons of his name.

* North Staffordshire dialect for 'You are sinew-tight': exhausted.

Note
Peter Reading's poem, *Dog's Tomb,* (Untitled, 2001) contains the lines, 'QVI CAECVS
ET SENECTVTE CONFECTVS. Who blindness and senility prepared'.

Rosita Sweetman

After the trip to the river

After the trip to the river
You made it clear,
Standing outside on the cold pavement,
The plashings were over.

Slamming face first
Into the plate glass
Of your decision,
I fall and fall.

Squeaking a goodbye
I head up the street
As if into a gale,
scalp numb
wet hair turned to glass.

I clutch my scarf to my neck.
My love. *My love!*

Vuyelwa Carlin

Rev. Fiddes Eradicates Infant Tetanus from St. Kilda

To show the uncertainty with which a woman regarded the life of her child ... she
rarely provided any clothing until the eight days had passed ...
Under Dr. Turner of Glasgow, Fiddes took a course in midwifery ...
                    Tom Steel, *The Life and Death of St. Kilda*

He was a tough character, loved his people;
his God, a builder; prayer a working, endless,
of hard materials; human endeavour's
utmost stretch – the cracking muscle tapping the divine.
His predecessor, John Mackay, banned storybooks,
and the old songs – eerie, in minor keys,
echoing cry of seabird, singing seals.
– So many men were lost: gale-pitched

with their bird-snares, down from the dizzy cliffs,
or tossed from little boats to the sudden-
madding sea. – And the babies, dying,
and dying, their jaws clamped? – why,

your wickedness, he said, and they believed him.
Sickness of eight days, the rag-wrapped mite:
– Fiddes, armed with antiseptic powder,
preached, cajoled; tangled with the old women,

and dead Mackay. – They'd hurried, eyes cast down,
to church three times each Sabbath: – poor greybeard,
rocking, dozing, in the roar of word,
of wind – *No sleep for you,* Mackay would shout,

in the next world! – But Angus Fiddes
prevailed. The deaths stopped. That plague, though,
had broken them – they were too few,
and stayed too few; forty years on, they left

(how sparse their bundles) that volcanic dot,
shield-shaped in the wild sea: the soaring
backless hills, scoured buttresses,
all white with birds; scoop, flail, of wind, and wave.

Rabid Boy

Aged, calm, she spoke
of far-off things: Gold Coast times,
her bat-bitten child,

growing ever more feverish
spasming horribly,
at the sight of water. The doctor

drove through the night – they were lone,
pressed in by jungle – *gave him something,*
she said, *to help him*

fall asleep: no-fuss
cessation – God be thanked – a grave
untorturing – though lost – cross

eaten away, small bones
surged through
with the riotous pungent Tropics, shrilled-

over by cicadas; heard yet, heart-
drilling, through her north-lit,
ninety-year-old nights.

St. Kilda Lament

Visitors to St. Kilda were struck by the lack of children on the island ... Tetanus
Infantum took its heavy toll.

Tom Steel, *The Life and Death of St. Kilda*

The sickness of eight days: Finlays,
Rachels, Euphemias, sleep with the rest
encircled by this wind-fluting dry wall.
– Knee-women's stubborn rites: the newborn's cord

was dressed in oil of fulmar, ruby-red,
bacillic, stored in a dried gannet's stomach.Years
of words, damnation-laced,
from Reverend John Mackay: diminutive,

in his tall hat, he stands on that bird-screamed,
far Hebridean speck, its giant stacks,
the mobbing seas. *This sickness
is from the Almighty,* the new-fangled nurse

(a pitching voyage she'd had of it) was told.
– The Evacuation, 1930: scatter
of bareoot children, ancients; the bird-catchers,
cliff-clamberers, mostly gone. All the dogs

were drowned – dozens, washing round Village Bay
for weeks. The everlasting wind
soon crumbled Village Street. The thousand
thousand birds whirl, swoop – the huge unhunted gannets

fiercer now. – Storm-beaten names
are almost flush with stone; small lockjaw bones,
tumbled from scrappy boxes (no trees here),
spread, split, beneath the whishing grass, wild sheep.

Note:
[1] A 'knee-woman' presided at a birth.
[2] The fulmar is a sea-bird, and formed a large part of the St. Kildans' diet. The oil was
used for lighting, cooking and as an all-purpose medicine.

Caroline Smith

Dr Modric

He steered the wheelbarrow
of damp mowings
round the bend in the garden path.
Always there,
in the corner of his eye
the cankerous weight of the compost heap
pressed through the wire mesh cage.
Like a heavy shouldered bison
it had leaned its depressed pelt
against him for nine years.
He stabbed his fork
into the dark overhang,
just as a break of sun,
like a token of grace,
rippled over its back.
It couldn't help but lift him,
like the rumour of the amnesty had
when for weeks he imagined he already
held the document in his hands –
flimsy hearsay that had filled out
the muscles of his dreams
set a million buffalo
pounding the vast prairies again.

Jeremy Page

Postcard of Odessa

Clearing out another drawer,
I come across the postcard
quite by chance – sepia, faded,
the city's name in Cyrillic script,
and before I know what I am doing
I am composing your name
in characters that are as unfamiliar
to me now as you are,
forty odd years on from the picnic
on the Potemkin steps, the glasses
raised to toast our futures
in the cheapest Soviet vodka;
and all the innocence you coaxed
from me, so tenderly.

John Buckley

Man's Best Friend

Sometimes he stops taking his meds since
he can't remember the taste of his tears.
So he cuts out the little pills for two weeks
or so, unhooks his blood from the leash,
and lets it scamper as it may, lets it drag
whatever chemicals it wants back home.
He becomes more playful, more willing
to leap up after spinning tropes. His coat
becomes sleeker; his appetite returns as
he also loses some weight. But after
a while, it once again has him snapping
at invisible strangers, furiously chasing
his tail and trying to bite it to the bone.
It's time for the muzzle to come back on,
a handful of milligrams daily forever.
He was never much of a crier anyway.

Stuart Medland

Beehive Huts

(from 'Skelligs')

Every hut
        is like the back of a man bent to enter, the

Mind of a man
          intent on his labour; knees

Drawn up to his chin, foetal
with eking his comfort from

Solitude's counsel in God's

Cold mammary.

Corbelled by slates, once
overlapping then always, like
waves retching in from the Sea.

Pimples of old Christianity.

Swimming the Horses

(from Mull to Iona)

To learn its ropes –
its land-legs gone, its
spirit broken once again –

A horse would need to
tread the mile of sea
between two islands.

All its wild-eyed terror
at the water thus contained;
its locomotive thrashings

Dissipated to a ripple
riding up a pebble on
a distant shore, the

Crossing, self-negotiated.
Better than a rowing boat
with hooves then legs

Through splintered
planks and swimming
anyway, a wooden ring

Around its flanks –
Men lost at sea.

William Bedford

Wagon & Horses

Grantham: 1947

At night I hear the revellers in the yard,
soldiers home from war, girls on their arms,
the clink of bottle tops on cobbled stone.
In restless sleep I lead my beer patrol.

They might be back from Napoleon's wars,
the drunken soldiery no longer dead,
horses or a child's dream of horses,
a harmless kind of cavalry charge.

The night is stars and planets wide,
as the yard of the *Wagon & Horses*
is wide, welcoming the homeless home.
They stumble legless across rough fields,

ghosts of the mud of the Great War,
veterans of Dunkirk's scoured dunes.
In the slap of river water down the road
they hear the frozen waves of German seas.

And I hear dolls in the darkness talking,
whispering their news of dolls' houses,
gossip like minnows and tiddlers
truer than the morning's raw headlines.

Saint Edith

There is no village where St Edith lies:
Coates-by-Stow an empty field
and copse of trees,
the racketing of crows the only choir.

In barley fields,
Cromwell's ghostly riders clatter by,
the chancel, nave and bellcote
crouched in frosted fear.

Where children used to play,
old women weep
for treasures lost on dusty shelves,
relics sold for gold.

The farm has gone.
The priest has left his beads.
The Corpus Christi guild's long closed.
Still, the lady knows:

above the rood screen's loft
a painted figure smiles:
warm light on wooden panelling,
rose windows broken rainbows.

Fishing

Tiddlers and minnows in the freshwater tub
stank the yard out for days. 'Damned child,'
the spinster next door complained.

How did we catch them? With a rod and net,
dredging the river's fast-flowing water,
leaning out over the edge.

The mud brought them up, churning sunlight.
We must have caught hundreds,
a living graveyard packed tight together,

swimming in the depths of the freshwater tub.
My mother belted me and sent me to bed,
but not for the smell in the cobbled yard:

she liked to wash her hair in fresh rain water,
fallen like a blessing from the clean skies.
When we moved away, we left the net behind.

Tim Liardet

Self-Portrait as Extreme Human Empathy

Those monstrous machines at daylight ripped out all the trees;
they ripped out tree after beloved tree, they ripped out all *your trees;*

all day they tore up roots, the great iron mouths got a hold, they left
enough stench of sickly sap adrift to make the air unbreathable.

The little wood in which you lived began to get smaller, and smaller;
like something would be exposed, was waiting to be shown

but no one knew what it was that crouched at the centre
like the New England animal, whatever it was, trying to panic a way out

of the wood's shrinking cover, heart straining on its stalks.
The machines might slaver and snort, you say, but they rip up

less the trees than the roots of your nerves... Love, its long
compassionate fingers, brain into genome. They get a hold. Your trees, your trees,

because they are the terrible upending of your own despair,
start to drop all around me. They fall. I fall. I fall again

and again. Every time the great mouth twists, rips out,
I fall. The teeth of the blades, as the revs drop, slice through my midriff,

cut me cleanly in two. The two halves, in equal measure,
hate the machines. They're like the worms, chopped orifice from orifice.

I am hacked bark, brutalized. I am chain-bruise, wrenched root,
I am dumped nest. Intricate fibers crying out inaudibly. I am

the stooping bough broken, chewed up. I am blood-pain, ravage and insult.
I am the snapping of root stems, trying to grip, grip. I am

your central nervous system, unable not to hear. I am your poor nerves
and the roots, untangling. Green sap. New root. Bud.

Self-Portrait as Biomolecular Love

Were there anything at all that could transubstantiate mass
it would sit at the chequered table. We were reminded how it struck

the light, our papers dishevelled all over it. We said: *a table!*
It drew us like food. Like a smell. Like promise. Like deprival.

It was the chequered table. We knew. Oh, our biomolecular love
would grow, couple with the molecules. Might become one thing

joined by a flat, seeming-not-to-move surface. Might be a cloister,
a piazza. A table. Our colloquy. Our atoms of gabfest and wood.

Our skin. Our shivery molecular want. Our dwelling-place. As if
our biomolecules, lipid and sterol, became it. As if the table cleared

a space in us, so we could clutter it. As if solitude was no longer
solitude, but ache conjoined. By the time we last reached across it

the table was wholly inside us, our groins its worldly root,
our spines its finitude, feet its feet. Beneath us we seemed to spread

its surface at our fingertips – a square comprised of smaller squares.
We sit at it for minutes, or for hours. Sometimes it is enough

to touch it just the once, idle a little finger along an edge,
leave a sheeny arc in the dust. The chequered table calls us forward, calls us back.

Our papers slew across it, will slew. Our cups make rings, draw light.
Our strangled voices at first sound strange, will sound less strange.

The chequered table loves – will love – our chaos. It gives
to our chaos a higher order, to higher order, chaos. It settles – will settle –

on our papers. It sits at us.
The chequered table will not want to sit at anyone but us.

Alison Brackenbury

The only end

Peter Dale: *Aquatints: New Poems 2012-2015* (The Minilith Press, 2015)
Hugo Williams: *I Knew the Bride* (Faber, 2014)
Clive James: *Sentenced to Life* (Picador, 2015)
Felix Dennis: *I Just Stepped Out* (Ebury Press, 2014)
Sebastian Barker: *The Land of Gold* (Enitharmon, 2014)
Dannie Abse: *Ask the Moon: New and Collected Poems 1948-2014*
(Hutchinson, 2014)

The six books in this review include three collections by poets whom I met, whose work I valued, and who are now dead. As I read all six collections, the rhythms of another poet's lines began to mutter in my head, strengthening into the bleakest music. The poet was Philip Larkin. The lines were the end of 'Dockery and Son':

> Life is first boredom, then fear.
> Whether or not we use it, it goes,
> And leaves what something hidden from us chose,
> And age, and then the only end of age.

After Larkin's savagery, it was a relief to meet the milder tones of the opening poem of *Aquatints*, Peter Dale's new collection. The colloquial, familiar voice of 'Wild Goose Chase' calls back an early landscape, 'a bit of road, left to an earth path', and its risks, 'the sewer pipe for river bridge'. These unpretentious details of the writer's childhood can link, intimately, to the reader's own life. Movingly, Dale shifts from the childish excuse 'Not me' to an adult's realisation: 'It wasn't me [...] it was everyone's'. Dale's poems of memory and reflection move from the viewpoint of a 'clever child' to a 'distance', open to silence, time and loss.

The best poems of *Aquatints* are lit by freshness and insight. Many poems have been written about family photographs. But how acutely Dale catches the separateness of three brothers, photographed together:

> We have no second sight
> to see their inner weather
> each gaze a changing light.
>   'Sorting Old Photographs'

101

The opening of 'Grace Notes' compels by very simple shifts: 'We were together there. We were together then'. I enjoyed Dale's puns, such as 'good-wink' for 'hood-wink', in a brief poem about the impossibility of a phone call from the dead. I also admired his sense of form, set against disintegration, and the boldness of informal speech within the poems. Dale's technique is high-risk, with an occasional lurch of metre, the odd word too obviously chosen to rhyme. But the successes of *Aquatints* are striking.

Dale's summaries verge on the savage: 'Books took our life'. 'Retroscope', one of his finest poems of the long view, turns upon sharp, rhyming phrases. It is an unforgivingly accurate memory of students dressed in their finery to go out: 'Too cold for that.' 'It was always too loud.' Realising their power, Dale isolates these observations as single lines. They take time's pulse. The prognosis is not good.

As with Hardy's poems of age and death, the poems' best hope is their own sound: '*Still here; do you hear?*' I was particularly moved by Dale's poem about a woman (his mother?) singing at night, with the undertow of an older music in a lilting half-line: 'She sang west Wiltshire tunes'. Poetry can salvage. What remains in the end is music.

The mental tunes set up by a collection's title can sound very different by its end. Hugo Williams' *I Knew the Bride* sounds a wickedly good, if slightly troubling title. This reviewer was charmed out of wariness by the first page:

> The day is difficult to start.
> I leave it at the top of a hill
> the night before. Next morning
> I release the handbrake
> and the whole rickety contraption
> chokes itself back to life.
>
> 'New Year Poem'

I admire the terseness, the airy casualness of the 'rickety contraption.' But there is menace in 'chokes'. Williams' wit is a bridge to darkness. The existence described in 'New Year Poem' may be a book 'with footnotes on the subject of desire'. But it flashes out uncomfortable questions: 'Is it too late/ to do something useful with my life?'

In 'Soul Singer', the speaker notes, unsurprisingly 'I'm not a demonstrative singer'. But the poem ends by repeating its opening line, with a surprising intensity. 'Can you hear me singing?' As I read Williams, Larkin became drowned out by Duke Ellington: 'It Don't Mean a Thing if It Ain't Got That Swing'. There is often a swing to the lines of this book. In 'Hotel' (another ominous title) 'Our room was a summer birdcage/ swinging from a hook'. Are the protagonists the same in 'Back and Forth'? 'She is sitting in the middle of her floor, / rocking'.

Understatement only throws into relief the grimness of many of Williams' subjects. 'The Work' does not refer to a poem, or a job, but surgery. The poem's work is to pare past pain and fear to fact: 'piercing the bony wall/ of the skull, just above my right ear'. Williams' greatest tenderness is often reserved for death. Gravestones – originally piled up by a young Thomas Hardy – stand around a tree 'like children listening to a story'.

The last poems in Williams' collection form a sequence based on his experience of kidney dialysis. As the machines' alarms go off, in a ward compared to the Grand Canyon, 'the whole/ hopeless blind herd/ is clip-clopping off into the sunset'. The poem is saved from the canyon of 'hopeless' by the levity of rhythm, the fantasy of a happy ending. Humour has its own final music.

Sadly, I discovered that I was right to be apprehensive about Williams' title. His poem, 'I Knew the Bride' is dedicated to 'my sister Polly 1950-2004'. But its title is taken from a song, and Polly is given a defiant exit: 'I saw the parting down the back of your head/ as you marched out of the room'. Bare of the consolations of rhyme, 'marched' carries Polly forward on the swing of her brother's line. In the collection's last poem, 'Prayer Before Sleeping', Williams asks 'Send me a poem, God'. I sympathised, charmed to the end, not even suspending disbelief for the final line, 'and I promise I'll be good.'

Sentenced to Life was written after Clive James was diagnosed with terminal leukaemia. But there is no trace of weakness in the title poem which opens this new collection. Its metrics are kept on a tight rein, as controlled as the fish in the 'goldfish pool', who never collide in their 'Trajectories as perfect as plain song'. Yet sense runs urgently between stanzas:

> I would lie
> As if I could be true to everyone
> At once, and all the damage that was done
>
> Was in the name of love, or so I thought.

Internal rhyme is a marker for the heightened sensitivity to 'Japanese anemones/ So pale, so frail.' Bare fact is equally telling. In the urgency of illness 'I count the bees'. James' strongest lines are often in two parts. Brevity focuses; his shortest stanzas are packed with meaning. He is at his best when pitting his energy against a poem's formal constraints, mirroring the inescapable demands of illness.

James' wit remains ferocious: 'You were the ghost they wanted at the feast,/ Though none of them recalls a word you said'. There are lines of bitter beauty: 'Burned by the starlight of our lives laid bare'. The possible smoothness of the pentameter is often disrupted by a jolt of alliteration, a lively insistence upon joy: 'As I lie restless yet most blessed of men'. This is a poetry of vital instruction: 'Steer clear of the cold air'. Like Pope and Johnson, James is never afraid of a memorable maxim: 'Remember liberty, and what it cost'. He is right to be fearless, although his courage may isolate him from his contemporaries.

But illness does not insulate James from life outside. He proudly retains his double vision of 'the English autumn' and Australia, 'the light I never left behind'. Australia echoes through his work, in 'the whip-bird's call' in 'Echo Point'. His eye is trained fiercely on a warring world, as in a poem about the wife of the President of Syria: 'Asma Unpacks Her Pretty Clothes'. James' jokes still pack a punch and are instantly memorable: 'I should record that out of any five/ Pictures by Kogan, at least six are fakes'. ('Nina Kogan's Geometrical Heaven'.)

Who could steer amorous lines into elegy more surely than Clive James? The last poem of this collection draws upon words from Ovid. But 'Lente currite noctis equi', 'Run slowly, slowly, horses of the night', now becomes 'The horses of the night that run so fast'. It is a fitting summary of *Sentenced to Life*'s many paradoxes of bodily illness and imaginative vigour. After clarity, pain, and delight, James' eloquence deliberately ends, before mystery.

Before I read Felix Dennis' tenth collection, I remembered one particular audience. It was a paying audience, consisting largely of young men, seated at tables, noisily eating and drinking. None of them had ever been seen at a poetry event in that town. Felix Dennis, performing his own poems from memory, silenced, amused and moved them. This was no small thing.

I Just Stepped Out is dedicated to 'the Muse who came late'. Publication of this book came after Dennis' own death from cancer. His absorbing introduction refers both to sex and, at greater length, his planting of a forest. The book's first section draws together earlier poems. The best have a rueful, song-like quality:

Try not to forget

To pluck all the cherries
Chance will allow,
Take them and welcome –
I'm done with them now.
('I Plucked All the Cherries')

There is no veil between Dennis' best lines and the world, past or present, as in his account of Victorian London, 'its roads awash with shit and snow'. His terseness still touches the pulse of the daily news: 'The test is who we save.'

Dennis' unashamed directness and jaunty rhymes are not to everyone's taste. 'Take them and welcome'. I have always felt welcomed by Dennis' work. He had his own style of producing books, with lavish footnotes. I think many readers unused to poetry would find these engrossing (as I do). Can Victorian diction smother his lines? Are his rhythms sometimes too slick? Yes. But his references to popular poets of the early twentieth century, such as Kipling and Henley, are thought-provoking. So is his statement: 'The post-World War II generation in the West (especially men) found it difficult to express their feelings'. I grew up in that silence. I agree. Remembering the enthralled (and relieved) faces of the young men who reacted so warmly to his poetry, I think that Dennis' comment remains true – especially of men. Poems as clear and unashamedly emotional as those of Felix Dennis keep a special value in British culture.

'What do we owe the dead [...]?' Dennis' reflections on his final bouts of illness are compelling: 'My next thought was: I have so little time'. 'There are no second acts except in plays.' 'I am writing two letters I know I'll destroy.' The references to anxieties about business, 'that debt/will sink our fledgling start-up', are intriguing, and too rare in poetry.

But a dying millionaire has other concerns: 'I have given my dog to a friend'. Dennis' poems are equally passionate about animals and trees: 'ash and oak/ And poplar'. I think this admirable, and a major reason why his poems engaged his audiences. His last work catches, memorably, the pathos of a very rich man amongst his useless possessions, the 'books I own but now shall never read'. The word that echoes, through poem after poem, is 'alone'.

Felix Dennis' poems never lose his enthusiasm for 'Life's mess'. Dennis claims to have overcome many addictions, and I believe him. But I find it hard to believe anyone would ever have weaned him off capital letters. And I still remember with amused approval his declaration that he a) had made his bank sponsor his current poetry tour and b) would spend all its profits on planting more trees.

I only heard Sebastian Barker read once, decades ago. But I have never forgotten the beauty and exuberance of the poems he read. He died in 2014. Today, outside my window, the buddleia is full of butterflies. On my screen are pages of quotations I have typed from Barker's radiant final collection. How do you choose between the Tortoiseshell's turquoise and the Comma's flame?

The Land of Gold is equally generous in its variety. Barker's briefest lines can capture cosmic energy: 'Scorpio rising/ In a great wheel'. They can also present truth as bleak as Larkin's:

> The love
> Of God soaring
> As the knives of the Vikings
> Went in.
>
> ('Skellig Michael')

One of Barker's most individual gifts is making the abstract flesh in poetry, as in 'The Grand Duchess of Philosophy': 'In the poem of Parmenides I saw her/ Standing in all her glory by the open door.' This long, spacious book is an open door, whose unrhymed poems, and lines without true rhyme, seemed to me to focus best, with Mediterranean clarity, on Barker's subjects.

His poetry does not ignore effort. The cicada is 'sawing words of praise'. An ecstatic response to the natural world, in its smallest detail, is one of the enduring delights of this collection. While showing compassion for 'a horse's tender eyes', plagued by flies, Barker's observations often beautifully combine the man-made and the natural: 'between the trees I go/ Treading tiles of sunlight on the grassy road'.

The poems of *The Land of Gold* gave me unforced, unfolding pleasure, especially in their accounts of Greece, where, Barker notes, he restored a ruined house at Sitochori. This landscape is summoned in the luminous colours of its 'golden-eyed goats', with humour and humility. 'Cicadas are the typists in the trees, writing it all down correctly.' 'Psari protects its magpies, who hop from hope to hope.' In the long lines of 'The Sitochori Poems', even a non-Christian may glimpse Barker's God 'gently persuading us to see things more through his eyes'. The poem's moral landscape may throw up probing questions to its richest, but most troubled visitor: 'Where is your Florida now?'

Yet 'Heaven is all about us', immediately followed by 'the ice-cream van'. Barker's long visionary lines can be briskly up-to-date – 'Hang on to your laptops' – or practical and domestic: 'The sink was blocked with a question'. But the poems remain unfailingly generous, reconciled both to the speaker's present and past. 'The many cats embarrass my door. There is nothing to do but feed them.' 'The places where we went together are warm with memory.'

Death enters Barker's book, burningly physical: 'the fragile icicle melts in its hot hand'. Yet, in humorous shifts of scale, it can make 'Tectonic plates tremble' then come 'so close, it nudges at my teacup'. Barker's last page states calmly that 'the closer you are to death' the more 'miraculous' the world appears. The vitality of *The Land of Gold* reminds us that bleakness is not our only end.

Finally, although I have reviewed Dannie Abse's poems elsewhere, I must briefly, but very warmly recommend *Ask the Moon,* his *New and Collected Poems*, published just after Abse's death in 2014. This includes his unforgettable 'In the Theatre', the description of a brain operation, when, under local anaesthetic, the patient cried out:

> and the words began
> to blur and slow, '...leave...my...soul...alone...'
> to cease at last when something other died.
> And silence matched the silence under snow.

I heard Dannie read this poem, with calm authority, at sixty. Thirty years later, I listened to him again. His only concession to age was to read from a chair. Inspiringly, the poems he wrote in his eighties seem to me amongst his best, fierce in politics, tender in love, celebrating the triumphs of daily life in his story of a seemingly futile journey through Wales:

> On schedule, at the terminus of Llantwit,
> the bus arrived empty, yet terrific with light.
>
> ('The Bus')

The poems of Abse's old age are, in the colloquial sense of the word, terrific. *Ask the Moon* covers at least fifteen collections. Even if (enviably) you own them all, do buy this book. You will find new poems at its moon-lit end.

Martyn Crucefix

Risk-takings

Colette Bryce: *The Whole & Rain-domed Universe* (Picador, 2014)
Janet Fisher: *Life and Other Terms* (Shoestring, 2015)
Claire Crowther: *On Narrowness* (Shearsman, 2015)
Tim Liardet: *The World Before Snow* (Carcanet, 2015)
Sheenagh Pugh: *Short Days, Long Shadows* (Seren, 2014)

Few recent books suggest the care with which they have been put together as much as Colette Bryce's *The Whole & Rain-domed Universe*. This helps the collection play cunningly with changes in perspective. An epigraph quotes Graham Robb suggesting that Rimbaud was attached to his origins 'by a powerful piece of elastic' and the implication is that Bryce herself, though firmly attached to her origins in the troubled north of Ireland in the 1970s, has swung near and far from it, up close and at a distance. The hyperbolic image of the whole and rain-domed universe is, of course, a child's eye view of the narrow and constricted world of childhood as template for the nature of the whole universe. A mistaken belief – only revealed as such when the child ventures out and away. 'Derry' traces some of this process in four sections of irregular quatrains (the poem is modelled on MacNeice's 'Carrickfergus'). The balladic form leads to some marvellous lines as well as some clumsy moments (even if the latter are intended to present the gauche child, I'm not sure it works). But the poem takes us vividly from the un-individuated child in the shadow of Derry cathedral, through encounters with British soldiers at checkpoints, the era of Thatcher and hunger strikes, the muting of Gerry Adams' voice on TV, to Bryce's exit to England and higher education. The latter moment – as the elastic tether stretches further than ever – has the homeland growing 'small' till it cannot be seen 'clearly anymore'.

Questions of perspective come into play in many following poems. Despite the politics, there is a warmth of nostalgia for the home though also a recognition that the milieu was boring and constricted. Bryce's grandmother's comment on the international success of Brian Friel's play *Philadelphia, Here I Come!* is simply to remark with pleasure at 'a Derry man / getting on'. But with escape comes distance and objectivity conveyed through the figuring of people as dolls (in 'Hide-and-seek' and 'The Brits'), the descriptive tone of the natural history programme ('The Republicans') or a scientific observer ('Positions Prior to the Arrival of the Military').

Distance here is not the same as detachment and the impact of these strategies on the reader is strongly emotional, evidently political, a record of a particular moment in history as well as autobiography. 'A Clan Gathering' documents the interactions at an extended family party, the traditional focus on heritage, gene pools, the 'excitable flow of births, / deaths, accidents, marriages'. But the narrator stands outside this with the unmentioned/ unmentionable presence of her gay partner who will never register in the 'great / genetic military campaign' of family. Such a poem reaches the realms of social satire in its distancing but it is followed immediately by 'Mammy Dozes' and it is the maternal figure who dominates most of the book. Here she sleeps, quietly, now intimately observed, like 'a boxer in defeat'. Seemingly subject to domestic violence, having given birth to nine children, her sleep is not merely defeat but a stoical resilience that – in other ways, in other realms – her daughter will have to take on.

Janet Fisher's poems have been noted for the amount of 'stuff' they contain (Peter Sansom) and her trust that such stuff plainly evoked for the reader will sufficiently convey what she wishes (Mimi Khalvati). Her titles tend to reflect such plainness with 'Advent, 'Actuality', 'Invitation' and 'Valentine' appearing in the opening six poems. Several of these are obliquely concerned with war as is 'A Roman Icon Ponders its Duty' in which a statue placed on 'a rock between latrines' laments its journey to Britain, far from the Roman sun and scent of 'sweet oregano'. It is ignored by the soldiers, at least until they receive bad news from home. This turning away from religious consolation seems to be a concern of Fisher's though – as here – the gesture towards it is not taken much further. The book has an interest in history too, though mostly in personal, often familial terms. 'No. 6' (the Players cigarette brand) has a shaky piano being played and nostalgically recalls the scratchy stink of Izal toilet paper, the whiff of sulphur from steam trains. But community is swiftly deconstructed when the matriarchal 'grandma' dies. There is also a 'Village Outing' on coaches to Wicksteed Park, this time with the whiff of "Woodbine" cigarettes but with a similarly packed programme of food, singing and old money denominations. The poems flaunt their working class credentials somewhat but they do succeed in evoking a world long since lost.

So it's disappointing that Fisher's insistence on plainness sometimes yields nothing but inconsequence as in 'Invitation' which is just what it says, promising homemade soup, bread and raspberries to eat. It wants to echo Williams' 'This is just to say' but fails to rise to its elegant line-breaking and sensual evocation. 'Voyagers' is an address to garden slugs as 'night seekers' and doesn't entertain, or transform, or avoid anthropomorphising the poor creatures. 'Praise' is a much better poem, listing in vigorous brief phrases all kinds of things on the principle of the opening line: 'Corners you go round not knowing what's there'. The title poem has the narrator gardening, layering, re-potting and finding in these actions a parallel with a life lived with 'no true and perfect implements', we must make do with 'only working usages'. Life then is not merely a term of nomenclature but also a period of incarceration. 'Birthday' concludes the book on a rather more redemptive note (and a more syntactically adventurous one too) with the flow of water from a tap, the sounds and scents of 'cool June' which encourages, 'my heart stretches, / a landscape / soaking up rain'.

Apart from the fierceness with which her poems corner from topic to topic and from one syntactical manoeuvre to another, there's ironically not much narrowness in Claire Crowther's third collection, *On Narrowness*. The brief title poem itself gives little away: uncapitalised and unpunctuated, a generic 'we' is located between walls, like librarians between bookshelves, and hence movement for them is 'hard'. Why (apparently) caryatids should welcome the love of such figures I'm not sure. Balancing buildings on their heads, perhaps caryatids also feel there is little room for movement and so the two figures have a shared experience. It's not just this poem that presents the reader with challenges of comprehension though the opening poem, 'The Alices', warns clearly enough that Crowther is very interested in the playfulness of language, developing and transmuting Carroll's 'Jaberwocky' verses into a more modern setting. This is not a book that is easy to like as the narrative voices shift continually, settings are often barely sketched in, bits of language strike off one another (sometimes like flints making sparks, other times more like people crashing about in the dark), line breaks often interrupt as much as integrate and syntactical leaps abound. This can make for exciting reading but at other times words lie inertly on the page awaiting some electric shock of connectivity that this reader (at least) often feels unable to provide.

This is a shame as Crowther has an adventurous way with language, an experimental approach to form and some quirky perspectives on things. 'Captured Women' describes drawings of women 'with their mouths tight / Shut' who nevertheless are imagined speaking, questioning and challenging the observer. Initially, they ask why we should stand there gazing at them; latterly they ask themselves why they should hang there to be observed. 'Self Portrait as Windscreen' is just what it says with a good deal of punning on the clearness of glass and/or point of view, plus the poet's Christian name. The processes of glass-making are brought into play, hardening from soft, fired, laminated, eventually destined to be cracked, all these qualities acquiring in the whirl of image and syntax both physical and psychological dimensions. 'Opponent' seems unusually clear in its narrative as the narrator is undergoing an operation on her stomach, involving endoscopy. She imagines a wolf in her stomach, growling and threatening, though (as often with Crowther) what is true or imagined becomes more and more blurred: 'Surely there is not / a wolf. Some other. I must be guarded'.

Tim Liardet is not a confessional poet in the usual sense but *The Storm House* (2011) revolved around the mysterious death of his brother and his new book, *The World Beyond Snow,* is driven by an affair with an American poet. But no, these are not heart- and soul-baring poems at all; rather they are highly wrought, intensely made and shaped and (for more gossipy readers) I'm afraid we learn next to nothing about the affair or the lovers themselves. This is curious as Liardet has suggested the book ought to be read as a 'love-story'. Furthermore, the form chosen for the majority of the poems is the self-portrait with accompanying objects or other figures, though the link to the artist or the assorted others is often so tangential as to make the quirky, miscellaneous titles less than helpful. Liardet uses mostly very long lines of around 14/15 syllables, mostly in blank couplets and repetition as a very common rhetorical device so the reader gets sped along very quickly and there is a sense of passionate engagement created, appropriate to the excitement of an affair. Though the self portrait that does emerge is of a voice in love with its own clever, improvisatory fertility ('she' hardly gets a look in), perhaps this again reflects the thrill and energising qualities of the illicit.

But the book is too long and has few changes in dynamic range or tone. 'Self-Portrait with Drag-Field and Dark' occurs early in the book and suggests an early encounter: 'What began was begun at the dun, customary table / where all things must begin'. The rotund repetitions here carry the reader along, perhaps persuading us not to question why 'all things must' begin in this way. Earlier we are told 'you belonged to someone else; // you belonged to someone else, and so did I'. Important information – but the repetition seems unnecessary and the more this occurs in the book, less is gained from the excess. 'Self-Portrait with Grief-Parting as Shakespearean Precipice' alludes to Gloucester's attempted suicide near Dover though the poem suggests the fearful leap into illicit love is actually dangerous rather than an opportunity for self-knowledge. The whirling syntax and repetitions of 'Self-Portrait with Cylindrical Snowstorm and Tired Pony Playing' effectively suggest the way each lover's experience blends and blurs into that of the other. The long lines and bravura image-making begin to run out of steam latterly (and the loved woman fades even further from view) but 'Self-Portrait with Hiss and Rattle of Sleet' conjures vivid sound pictures of a snow storm, piling word on word as the flakes 'clatter and blitz, sizzle and rebound, parabola and skip' and metaphor: 'like grapeshot, // pure pelletry, like blasted grains. Like maggots bouncing'. This is the sort of thing the narrative voice insists on doing and though a brave book in many ways, Liardet's style hides as much as it reveals.

Sheenagh Pugh's *Short Days, Long Shadows* strongly bears the mark of her re-location in recent years from Cardiff to the Shetland Islands. There are a couple of leaving-taking pieces here with 'How to Leave' re-enacting the slow, even painful, notation of local detail and the levels of self-deception often accompanying what looks like a partly reluctant move. 'Ghosts of Cardiff' more reflectively argues that it is less the 'now' that proves so hard to turn away from, it is 'all the thens' which remain at least as vivid as any present moment. These hauntings form just one of the many sub-sets of 'Long Shadows' in this collection and Pugh's much-remarked sense of history is a further important manifestation of this too. But it is the northern landscapes that dominate the book, the Shetlands and Scandinavia. 'Big Sky' makes the scenic novelty clear when the gaze from a window meets 'no branch, no office block', but 'overflows with sky'. The breadth and variety of cloudscape and the bright night's 'cluster and prickle' of stars are vividly evoked yet the individual's humility before such a natural scene is undermined by a final line suggesting a yearning for 'the way out'. There is something of this reflected in the book's structuring where, instead of blockish sequences of related poems, individual pieces tend to bounce and ricochet off each other. Pugh's language risks becoming a little dull but I find this quality of restlessness in her work very engaging. It is a determination not to accept limits as in 'Living in a Snow Globe' where a northern blizzard again concludes with a small figure 'fixed in a shaking flux and unsure / where here is, or how to get out'.

Since she gave up the hostage to fortune that being judged 'too accessible' as a poet was the best sort of compliment, there has been much discussion of Pugh's plainness, simplicity, even her unchallenging art. It's true there are poems here that do little more than make a few well-turned observations, in plain language, in skilfully handled, mostly free verse. But I think – in the face of a pretty bleak view of temporal change – the stoicism which underlies much of her thought manifests itself in terms of lexical and formal choices as the desire to communicate truth as plainly as possible. There is surely something of this in the astutely placed opening poem, 'Extremophile'. The title refers to those life forms which, against all the odds, manage to carve out a life in extreme conditions around hydrothermal vents, in permanently darkened caves, in Antarctic valleys. It is this determination that Pugh finds inspiring: 'There is nowhere / life cannot take hold, nowhere so salt, / so cold, so acid, but some chancer / will be there'. Look at that brilliantly chosen colloquialism 'chancer' to suggest the risk-taking, against-the-odds, stubborn resilience of life itself that Pugh's human subjects more often than not also share.

David Cooke

Family Histories

Paula Meehan: *Mysteries of the Home* (The Dedalus Press, 2013)
Alison McVety: *Lighthouses* (SmithDoorstop, 2014)
Kerry Hardie: *The Zebra Stood in the Night* (Bloodaxe Books, 2014)

Born in 1955, Paula Meehan is a poet and dramatist who was appointed to the Chair of Ireland Professor of Poetry in 2013, a fact which may account for this timely reprint of *Mysteries of the Home*. First published by Bloodaxe Books in 1996, it is a distillation of the best of her earlier work from *The Man who was Marked by Winter* (The Gallery Press, 1991) and *Pillow Talk* (The Gallery Press, 1994). Born into a working class Dublin family, Meehan was by her own account a rebellious adolescent and something of a 'wild child'. In her prefatory poem, 'The Well' she makes use of an archetypal image to hint at the mysterious source of her poetry:

> *This path's well worn.*
> *I lug a bucket by bramble and blossoming blackthorn.*
> *I know this path by magic not by sight.*
> *Next morning when I come home quite unkempt*
> *I cannot tell what happened at the well.*
> *You spurn my explanation of a sex spell*
> *cast by the spirit who guards the source ...*

Although this is a poem which is atypical, perhaps, in its use of rhyme, fairly regular metre and its rural setting, it nonetheless hints at polarities that lie at the heart of Meehan's work: subservience and freedom; sensuality and repression; spirituality and organized religion. The image of the well as a source of poetry, rooted in a community and its oral tradition, is one that has been put to memorable use by certain other Irish language and Scots Gaelic poets – one thinks of Cathal Ó Searchaigh and Ruaraidh MacThòmais. Growing up in a home where there was little access to books or conventional 'literature', Meehan spoke movingly in an interview with the American poet, Michael Collier, in 2000 of how, as a child, she was surrounded by poetry in the street songs of her city and the stories she heard from her grandmother.

In 'A Child's Map of Dublin', we follow her as she walks 'the northside streets / that whelped me,' although the past is now irrecoverable: 'not a brick remains / of the tenement I reached the age of reason in.' This is, however, more than a mere exercise in nostalgia. In revisiting her roots, Meehan gives us an indication of the journey she has taken in moving beyond them. Her yearning for personal freedom is first expressed in the image of a gull; 'common cacophonist ... squabbler / of windowledges ... // nothing reads the wind so well;' and is foregrounded again in the poem's sensual conclusion:

Climb in here between the sheets
in the last light of this April evening. We'll trust
the charts of our bodies.

In 'Buying Winkles' one gets the impression of a childhood that is uncomplicated and secure in its sense of community:

I'd bear the newspaper twists
bulging fat with winkles
proudly home, like torches.

However, in 'Three Paintings of York Street' she creates an atmosphere that is less idyllic and one where life chances and, in particular, those of working class women are highly circumscribed. In '*Before the Pubs Close*' the painter is advised to 'Salt your canvas with a woman / quietly weeping in a tenement room.' In the second panel of her triptych, '*Woman Found Dead behind Salvation Army Hostel*', she pulls no punches in describing 'the eerie green of her bruises, / the garish crimson of her broken mouth.'

Meehan's natural inclination to speak up for those who are disenfranchised and impoverished has over the years been reinforced not only by observing at first hand the tough lives of her parents but also by the years she has spent leading workshops in women's prisons. Many of those incarcerated were victims of the heroin epidemic that ravaged Dublin in the 1980s. Her astonishing poem, 'Her Heroin Dream' is a tour-de-force and something quite new in Irish poetry:

The Liffey and the two canals would vanish
and Dublin bay evaporate, leaving beached
spiny prawns and crabs, coiled sea snails,
a dead sailor's shoe, shipping wrecks,
radioactive waste in Saharas of sand.
The buildings would scorch to black stumps,
bricks fallen to dust would sift
in dervish swirls along the thoroughfares.

'The Man who was Marked by Winter' is a powerful depiction of a suicide: 'His past is a blank / snowfield where no one will step;' while in 'The Statue of the Virgin at Granard Speaks' she evokes a landscape and its culture, but then homes in on one of its victims:

> On a night like this I remember the child
> who came with fifteen summers to her name,
> and she lay down alone at my feet
> without midwife or doctor or friend to hold her hand.

The poem ends on a note of paganism when the Virgin, an idealization of sexual repression, addresses the sun: 'burning heart of stone, / molten mother of us all, / hear me and have pity'. Elsewhere in the poem the statue's avowal of sexual longing is made explicit: 'My being / cries out to be incarnate, incarnate and tousled in a honeyed bed'.

Throughout these poems Meehan expresses her contempt for institutionalized Catholicism but, beyond that, there is an unabashed frankness in her handling of sexual themes. Frequently informed by an almost visceral feminism, her work as a love poet is nonetheless multi-faceted. In 'Not Your Muse' the tone is challenging in its refusal to fit the mould of masculine ideals: 'Can / you not see I am an ordinary woman / tied to the moon's phases, bloody / six days in twenty-eight?' 'My Love about his Business in the Barn' is a celebration of love that crackles with the burr of its homely diction:

> You're fiddling with something in the barn,
> a makeshift yoke for beans to climb,
> held together like much in our lives
> with blue baling twine, scraps of chicken wire.

By way of contrast, 'Not alone the rue in my herb garden' is a leisurely portrayal of domesticity from which, in the end, the woman moves away: 'O my friend, / do not turn on me in hatred, / do not curse the day we met'; while in 'Laburnum' it is the female protagonist who is left forlorn.

Whether she is describing her conflicted relationship with her mother in 'The Pattern', portraying her father 'as a vision of St Francis' or exploring the most unfathomable depths of her own sensuality in 'Pillow Talk', Paula Meehan's poems have the stamp of authenticity. Lyrical, impassioned, direct, they are utterly devoid of artifice.

Lighthouses, Alison McVety's third collection, extends and enriches what is fast becoming an impressive body of work. In her debut, *The Night*

Trotsky Came to Stay (Smith DoorStop, 2007) she made the urban landscape of Manchester and the North West her own in the way that Douglas Dunn had previously laid claim to the back streets of Hull. She also began her moving exploration of family history. While this subject matter is again much in evidence, she moves beyond it in a collection that is wide-ranging and sometimes challenging in the scope of its references and the subtlety of her approach.

However, in many poems we are on familiar territory. 'Departures' opens with a typically neat image: 'As the train leaves, the LED wipes out its past, / adjusts its future'. Then from the platform we view 'an ordered row of terraces' and get a sense of the lives lived there:

> From the street I hear food making its way
>
> to tables and beyond the doors, hallways
> are gridlocked with laptops, homework, shoes –
> all parked for supper, the hand-to-hand
>
> of pass-the-parcel meals.

'Semi-detached' is a vignette of cheek-by-jowl existence in which neighbours can't escape the minutiae of each others' lives: 'the after-pub sex / the telephone's rant / the cistern/s roar at a vindaloo'. Impressive also is the bleak vision of 'The Mile End Road at Midnight' in which 'midlife men / tear back from women they / do not love to wives they do not / know'; while in 'Crewe', which is brief enough to be quoted in its entirety, she evokes a sense of Northern roots surviving social mobility:

> they all came here to change
> hometowns slipped out of
> like winter coats
> accents thrown off
> in favour of lighter ones –
>
> and all the while grit
> pearling under the tongue.

Convincing and well observed, these are poems which would have slotted neatly into McVety's two previous collections. However, it is in her poems about her parents – her love for them and theirs for each other – that she writes with an emotional depth surpassing what has gone before. Here are the opening lines of 'Finlandia':

> What I know about death is Sibelius
> on the high fidelity music centre, dad
> listening in the dark, gas off, still
> in his wind cheater with corduroy trim:
> Sibelius so high it distorts the angles of the day;
> Sibelius until the street light's eye
> is replaced by a cold sun's watch,
> by which time my dad has remade my mother
> into a living woman.

McVety has always been at her best when writing about her family. In 'Light House' she is almost unbearable poignant: 'and there was an airiness / to those few moments // ... before he released his hand, was disappointed / that my face was not hers.' In 'The Light Fantastic' the luminous world of ballroom dancing is set against the backdrop of old age and the ravages it inflicts: 'tripping the light fantastic in the Tower Ballroom, hips / chassé-ing, thumb in the nub of her fancy man's arm.' Touching also are poems evoking the poet's adolescence and her relationship with her mother: 'White Jeans' in which mother and daughter know 'that white jeans were just the start of it;' and 'My Mother as the Lovell Telescope' in which, as if updating John Donne, she portrays her mother as a source of wisdom and sensitivity: '*Listen to the sky waves*, she says, *listen / to the pain of everything speaking at once*'.

Among her more challenging poems are a series of nine skewed sonnets beginning with 'Honeymoons'. Building up to an enigmatic narrative, they are defined by geographical locations that are sometimes precise: Dubai, Sheffield, Johannesburg and sometimes not: 'home', 'away', 'elsewhere'. Disorientating in the way that a *nouveau roman* might be, they are illuminated by dazzling images and flashes of insight. Describing the desert landscape of Dubai, the poet evokes 'fluid boundaries', and moves from 'this duned / skin of land' to zebras and 'the black and white' of a kiss'. 'Mallory', set in Sheffield, seems to be a dreamlike encounter with the legendary mountaineer 'in the thin air above the plains of Tinsley'. In a sequence of sharply focused images, 'Afterword' looks back on a marriage: 'What I remember is this: your mouth blowing / wet Os in the mizzled rain of the shower door'.

Time passing is also the theme of 'To the Lighthouse', one of several poems inspired by the work of Virginia Woolf and a worthy winner of the

117

2011 National Poetry Competition. In its opening section there is a sense of disappointment as the poem's protagonist has to sit an examination for which she is ill prepared:

> In the hall I watched
> the future show its pulse and all the girls,
> the girls who'd read the book, set off
> together, lined up at desks and rowing.

Then the years fly until, by the time she 'gave the book another go, (the year my mother died), she has 'learned / everything big happens in parenthesis – marriage, birth, the War.' McVety's most ambitious volume to date, *Lighthouses,* is intellectually challenging but emotionally satisfying. It will not disappoint those who admire her work.

Kerry Hardie's *Selected Poems,* published in 2011 by Bloodaxe Books, included work from five collections first published by the Gallery Press. It was followed almost immediately by *The Ash and the Oak and the Wild Cherry Tree* (The Gallery Press, 2012). Her seventh collection, *The Zebra Stood in the Night,* now appears just over two years later. Written in an attempt to come to terms with the loss of her young brother, Paddy, it is a heart-rending exegesis of grief and mortality. Divided into two parts, the poems in the opening section are wide-ranging, while those in its concluding section focus upon the death of her brother. Her opening poem, 'Conditioning' is a brief existential lyric which, like many of her poems, is pitch-perfect and resonates beyond its brief compass:

> It's all the stuff they taught us in our childhoods,
> the lessons hammered from their smelt of pain –
>
> insure, secure, and burglar-proof your cell,
> equip with all the smartest apps and trends.
>
> The future waits out there, pitch-black, unknown,
> beyond the knife-edge of the precinct lights.

Minimalism does of course have its risks and occasionally, as in her title poem, the words seem merely gnomic and promise more than they deliver. However, in 'How it Happens' she achieves more in six lines than many others might in as many stanzas:

Yesterday someone up there in the sky
threw down a bucket
of mist and green mud,
and the spring spilled out
in a wash of bright rain
and broken light, coming and going.

Slyly begging the big question, this is a poem which is utterly convincing in the physicality of its imagery and movement. Throughout her opening section Hardie's insights into the natural world are informed by her attempt to make sense of its cycles of death and renewal. The stripped back opening stanza of 'Leaf-fall' has a classical simplicity: '"Chestnuts are the stubbornest" / The pithy brown husks / that shielded the fruits / lie scattered about on the grass. / Also leaves. / But so many still on the trees'; yet there is a matter-of-fact inevitability about the trees 'letting fall / what they have no use for'. 'Sealed Vessel' is a marvellous poem about slugs which bears comparison with Thom Gunn's 'Considering the Snail'. The distaste expressed in its opening couplet leads, in the end, to an acceptance that these creatures, too, have their place in the scheme of things:

It is hard not to hate
glutinous black slugs,

hard to include them
in life when they mostly appear

to be eating it....

Maybe they are
earth's lead, the alchemist's base metal –

poisonous, deadweight. Yet somehow
essential.

Elsewhere, her descriptions of nature have the astringency of many of the Early Irish glosses. 'Song', evoking 'the old bell-sounds of the stag', is reminiscent of *Scel lem duib*; while 'November' seems to be self-consciously replicating its form:

119

Sheep cough,
limp fading grass.
Mud-prints in gaps
fill and glaze over.

While observation of the natural world may give the poet an oblique insight into human mortality, she explores it more directly in the elegies she has written for Dennis O'Driscoll, Seamus Heaney and several others. 'Threnody for Seamus' demonstrates that minimalism is not Hardie's only mode of expression and reminds us also that she is a novelist. It starts off mundanely enough: 'I've taken a sick dog to the vet and we're waiting', but soon expands into a seemingly casual accumulation of details, concluding that life is 'just a wriggle of light / that slips through your fingers'. Equally impressive is 'Report', replete with details of fields and beasts and the odds and ends of country life. Brilliantly orchestrated and richly textured, the fifty poems of Part One counterbalance the inevitability of decay against the beauty of the natural world, while the consolations of art and the rituals of community are seen, perhaps, as the only bulwark we have against our own mortality.

Having established this as the context in which she will explore her own feelings of loss, she opens Part Two with 'Aftermath', a prose meditation upon the subject of grief, which, she explains in her introductory note, 'is not specific to my brother's death'. The piece begins with a grotesque image. Having slipped and got stuck in a boghole, the poet comes into contact with the decomposing body of a sheep which, subsequently, haunts her with its 'death smell': 'I became obsessively conscious of it... I imagined the warmth of the room was increasing the smell and drawing it from my skin'. She then moves on to suggest that the material values of Celtic-Tiger Ireland have eroded the rituals that once helped to assuage our griefs and that now we are on our own: 'But the death-smell is in our nostrils and in our clothes and deep in the pores of our skin. Though strangers cannot smell it, we can smell nothing else'. Powerful, also, is her description of the 'yo-yo' effect of joy slowly returning, which then brings in its wake 'feelings of betrayal and hence the return of suffering'. The analytical prose of 'Aftermath' is followed by a sequence of lyrical and meditative fragments, which Hardie considers to be 'really one long poem' but which she has separated out 'to help the reader to understand the events behind them'. Some, such as 'The Door' and 'In San Vincente', are written in prose and expand the insights of 'An Aftermath', while others are more obviously poetic. The starkness of 'What's Left' is in marked contrast to the expository tone of 'Aftermath':

I do not move much beyond matter.
What is touched, seen, heard.

The stunned bird kicks in my hand.
I watch its eyes dull and glaze over.
It is mute, warm, dead.

Again, as in Part One, mundane life is seen as the backdrop to tragedy. Here are some lines from 'After You Died': 'If it hadn't been India / it would have been somewhere else... Perhaps I'm glad that your window / opened onto the market. / And over the road, the pigeons / ... lost in the roar from the street'. The prose poem' Your Box' is a forlorn account of transporting her brother's ashes back to Ireland, involving an awkward conversation with some Australian lads. In 'Thirteen Months' the poet is haunted by the ghost of her brother whenever she sees the bus that used to bring him home. However, it is in 'Child' that she is at her most poignant. As he tries to come to terms with his grief, her young nephew goes to bed each night surrounded by his father's clothes: 'After a while he put them back himself. His body / must have drawn from yours the strength it needed'. Understated and seemingly artless, *The Zebra Stood in the Night* is a moving and, at times, profound collection in which universal themes are viewed through the lens of private loss.

Patricia McCarthy

Ladies of the Light

Eiléan Ní Chuilleanáin: *The Boys of Bluehill* (The Gallery Press, 2015)
Breda Wall Ryan: *In a Hare's Eye* (Doire Press, 2015)
Jane Clarke: *The River* (Bloodaxe Books, 2015)

Eiléan Ni Chuilleanáin, the legendary doyenne of poetry, has to head this trio of women whose voices should not go unnoticed. Eiléan herself has been honoured with many prizes, not least the prestigious Griffin Prize (for her collection *The Sun-Fish* (Gallery Press 2012).

Eiléan is a poet who, in Keats's terms, practises 'negative capability'. Her poems that concern both time and timelessness live 'in the moving gondola of light' searched for by a mountain personified as 'a woman/ With the face of Achilles and the bare/ Shoulders of Andromache' in the poem 'Clouds' from *The Sun-Fish*. She has very much her own voice, her own transformative imagination and her unique way of telling, taking mysterious perspectives not always the most accessible, at first. Her work definitely repays reading and re-reading.

This latest collection from Gallery Press, *The Boys of Bluehill* (named after a tune 'with the lewd words added'), echoes quite obviously her previous prize-winning collection, with its disordering of order, its delving into the tricks of light and language, its summoning of strange, semi-real worlds that become our total reality as we read her lines. Indeed, the poems seem to create themselves. Her Irish nationality is used, not as a political weapon, but as an occasional springboard, with place-names, to reproduce a timeless, universally archetypal world in which anything can happen. Her poetry possesses the gift of making us see differently, of unsettling us while it intrigues with its potions of almost white-witching magic, and ominous endings.

The poem, 'In the Distance' describes a woman from Youghal with her 'crime novels,/ the cigarettes, the bottle of stout'..., where 'between// the boat and the land swam a vacant pool of light – /and beyond that absence lay a world, that was sold/ for huddling doubts and envies'. It is this 'vacant pool of light' that Eilean fills with worlds other than those obsessed with 'huddling doubts and envies' and we have her to thank for this.

She gives no back-story, little or no explanation of context, and the 'secretive ocean' she speaks of in a poem could be her own personal subconscious. Her world is very much a dreamer's, often surrealistic, with startling, almost Martian images surprisingly juxtaposed ('for example in *The Sun-Fish* 'The silk scarves/ Came flying at her face like a car wash'). She is not afraid of using her learning in her poetry and when she wants to strike deep into the heart, she does with ease (e.g. her two moving elegies to Pearse Hutchinson), though even these surprise; one contains a surreal dream landscape in a library; the other, entitled 'Small', focuses on Pearse's fascination, like her own, with languages:

> The small difference intrigued you,
> between a word in Catalan and its Castilian cousin;
> the dense closeness, the narrow gap
> distancing the genitive poural in Irish
> from the nominative singular,
> the narrow vastness between a broad and slender *r*:
> *fear, fir,*
> like a small woman reaching up
> to stroke a tall man's muscled shoulder…

As everywhere in her work, 'time is shuffled', the dead appear as 'gentle intruders/ wrapped in their whispers' or, eerily, have 'lips/ that move in the grave'. There are apparitions such as the girl with the full, embroidered skirt, holding a violin, who appears at the top of a staircase, then fades as 'the stairwell plunges away'. There are biblical scenes transformed into painterly visions in the poet's imagination, some lines of humour are thrown in; there are even what appear to be more 'personal' poems in this collection. These seem at times slighter, yet even there the mystery remains as to whether the 'I' in the poems is Eilean's own 'I' or that of an anonymous persona. A particularly memorable one is 'Direction' concerning re-finding her long-dead father who 'has moved and changed/ more than in all of his life'. He undergoes metamorphoses, becoming

> a sliding dance of peaks, their names picked from his list:
> the words remembered from the internment camp
> that gave him his phobia of candles, his cardplaying codes,
> the pipe he never smoked with its ivory bowl.

All in all, it is the 'light' in her poems that we remember, just as, in 'Witness'

The light when she remembered
after the storm had passed
was as clear as a day in Galway…

it fills her now with light
until she can't hold any more,
until her tongue cannot move.

A strong new voice, also on the other side of the Irish Sea, is Breda
Wall Ryan. Although a multi-prizewinning poet, *In a Hare's Eye* is her
first collection. Her haunting music, also at times surreal, uncovers the
vulnerability in all human lives. As Paula Meehan, Ireland's Chair of Poetry
says, '…to all that she sees, even in the darkest places, she brings the light
of her careful attention'. And this 'attention' is not only an illumination, but
is crafted with precision and insight, showing her to be a real wordsmith,
brimming over with startlingly accurate imagery and patterning. For example
in the poem 'If What is, is Other' the string of epiphanies is embedded
in a patterned repetition that catches the ear: in each four-line stanza, the
third line begins similarly but differently with ' I have tasted……', 'I have
felt.…', 'I have touched.…', 'I have tasted…', 'I have breathed…'.

Like Eiléan, Breda is a big poet, full of scope. She, too, is concerned
with language e.g. 'Self Portrait as a She Wolf' ends with the resounding
'Your throat opens/ on one, long, swooped syllable,/almost a word'. In
'Wake', her elegy for Seamus Heaney, the music of language is reassuringly
everywhere: there is the mix of 'spirit music', 'wave tunes', 'or the keening
of the shearwater,/ a soulbird singing home.' Parallels with Heaney arise
with her knowledge of flora and fauna and its texture; with her very moving
poem(s) to her mother on the farm, the poet a child:

I watched her white breaths,
her hands tearing feathers from flesh,
flurries of down drifting
around her head like bloodied snow,
catching on the straws and the barbs
of blackthorns.

Heaney peeling potatoes with his own mother is not so very far away.
Breda's mother 'became a wild thing, a merlin at her plucking post'.

At times, unlike Yeats who re-made old myths, and unlike Eiléan who
embeds classical mythology in her work, Breda constructs her own myths
such as in the clever poem,'Woman of the Atlantic Seaboard', a wild

woman who can be met 'anywhere on the coast', can be any woman and every woman in one:

> ...Call her by any of her names:
> she will turn from you to the blue nor'wester,
> shake brined beads from her hair. She will wait
> for her drownlings forever, standing in the salt rain.

The pathos here is very close to that in Matthew Arnold's 'Forsaken Merman' with which this poem bears a kinship. A similar universality is to be found in 'The Camel, Perfected' with wonderful images from around the world to define anatomically a horse in a kind of ancient, but timeless, litany, reminiscent of Taliesin: 'his cannonbones are Zulu knobkerries'and 'his fetlocks are the swaying grass skirts of Nubian maidens' – as strikingly original, this imagery, as Eiléan's. Her ekphrastic poems, too, such as her take on Mary Magdalene in 'Cailín Rua', are full of a lightly-worn learning and images culled from a wider civilisation than just that found in Ireland.

Ireland, too, however, is woven into the poems naturally, with 'The Laying of the Bog' hinting at Ireland's troubled history: 'Beneath Earth's coverlet of marled tweed/ lie bones of smothered farms and drowned fields'. Pain, also, is hauntingly articulated in her hospital poems. In 'Dear Surgeon, I imagine you' there is a weirdly effective mixture of the medical with the lyrical, while in 'Vanishing' the experience is that of most patients: being made anonymous despite a name-tag and recorded date of birth.

The more I read Breda's poems, the more I find to write about them, but, alas, have no more room. All I can say is that here is a gigantically-gifted woman poet who deserves careful attention and an essay on her work alone.

Irish poet, Jane Clarke's *The River*, published in England by Bloodaxe, has received great attention in Ireland, and, I hear, has topped, in Dublin, Hodges Figgis's bestseller list. The last poetry bestseller I can think of was Ted Hughes' *Birthday Letters*, so she is in good company. Here are much more simple, direct poems, delicately written, successfully encompassing daily rituals. Jane's typical Irish farm background is much more to the fore than Breda's, though the former does embrace other themes such as freedom: 'how we longed/ for the morning we'd shut the gate and walk away', letting go, loss, independence: trying to 'find a place in gravel and silt//to hollow a dip/ and spawn a life of your own'.

The Irish rural stuff has all been done before, in the mouths of male Irish poets, and it could be asked: do we need any more? However, it is refreshing at least when seen through the eyes of a – what traditionally has been silent – woman. She gives us snippets of life down on the farm, not particularly original, though she is very good at conjuring the past through lists or impressionistic details, e.g. the busy farmer is made alive by the line that summarises him: 'cigarettes, silage and Brylcream'. It must be her accessibility that makes her so popular, particularly with readers who do not live in the country; otherwise, to country dwellers, she can seem to be merely stating the obvious, and place-names slipped in could appear to be playing slightly to the gallery. Never mind; this is a poet who perhaps hasn't quite grown yet into her very best, who writes, for now, at her best when she goes beneath the surface and uses language-patterns.

Two very finely achieved poems are 'Kintsugi' and 'The Globe'. In 'Kintsugi' she cleverly uses the sustained image of the teapot to show that the person who had a serious accident in the poem has died. When she hears the news of his accident 'I let the teapot slip from my hands/ to terracotta kitchen tiles'. She hears more about the casualty and 'fitted' the pottery pieces 'together with glue'. But when she hears the worst, 'I found the teapot could not hold'. This is a clever way of distancing emotion, yet intensifying it. Her approach is similar in 'The Globe' which entails a childhood memory in a 'one-roomed school house down the road // where pupils brought a sod of turf / for the fire each day'. Having searched, with the other pupils for various countries on its circumference, she is given the privilege of carrying it to the master. Alas, it falls – 'a crack, a hush, a broken world rolls'.

Another successful poem is 'The Suitcase' which her mother kept packed: 'the nightie, toothbrush, nylons,/ miniature bible and summer dress' which meant 'it was herself// she was telling, I can go, if I want to'; the final line explains: 'it was the suitcase that helped her to stay'. Poems like these, when she skilfully uses extended metaphor, rescue her from a run of unremarkable lines that do occur occasionally, and from weaker poems that go nowhere.

'Every Life' is another movingly achieved poem in which the persona is desperate to have a child. It broadens out to embrace all childless women everywhere who stop themselves 'thinking of names, Oisin, Molly, Sineád'. The final poem in the collection, 'The River', is simply said but what we all want to say and, as such, very moving. It is a universal poem of loss in which the persona at last manages to move on and call herself 'free', despite the fact that at times 'the river flows backwards, uphill to my door'. Here, like many other poems, Jane proves she is very gifted at endings that ring on after the poem is finished.

Breda Wall Ryan says, 'There's always a song on the wind'. Let us hope therefore that these three 'Ladies of the Light' continue to find such songs and sing them to all of us forever after.

CHOSEN BROADSHEET POETS

Ben Parker was born in Worcester in 1982. In 2012 his debut pamphlet, *The Escape Artists*, was published by tall-lighthouse. He is currently poet-in-residence at the Museum of Royal Worcester.

How She Remembers

On the rare occasions
when she walks in woodland alone
the muffled blows
of a distant woodpecker
bring back no memories
of her grandmother, pausing
mid-step, head cocked
and thin arm raised like a bare branch,
signalling the sound of her favourite bird;

nor does the smell
of freshly brewed Costa Rican coffee
remind her of her father
back from his year-long 'indiscretion'
in a mountain village,
tamping the grounds like gunpowder
and making her try just one more time
that drink for which
she never developed a taste.

But if she steps outside
slightly underdressed for the year's
first crop of snow
she is back at her mother's house
and the frozen week she spent
rising an hour early
and lifting the lid of ice
from all the neighbours' ponds
to allow the fish to breathe;

and at the height of summer,
when the office air conditioning failed,
she stared at her cubicle wall
and saw the beach
where she lost an afternoon
burying all the watches she could steal
so everyone might remain
where they were, lying
in that heat forever.

The Key

When he died and we finally summoned the courage
to open the locked drawer in his office, we needed
first to force it, his set of keys having also disappeared
as if buried in the coffin with his body dressed for work.

Once inside we did not discover the pornographic stash
we'd feared, the illicit letters of our salacious guesses,
the half-finished bottle of our noirish ones. Instead
it was simply this: the key to the lock we had prised

and no doubt broken in the process. There was no
mistaking it, all of us had seen it quickly turned
each time we entered unannounced this room
of his retreat. Had he known he was going to die

and hidden the contents elsewhere, or burned them,
leaving a copy of this key as reprimand? Or was
this drawer, sealing in its snug coffin the means
to its own release, his final message? Had all those

sudden furtive lockings been a ruse to bring us here?
To show perhaps that certain secrets are secret only
for the sake of holding something back. That if we keep
nothing else from those we love we should keep that.

Kevin Graham lives and works in Dublin. Born in 1981, he has a
BSc in Applied Computational Linguistics. His poems have appeared in
various journals such as *Acumen*, *Magma*, *Stand, The Shop,* as well as the
Templar anthology *Peloton*. In 2012 he was selected for the Poetry Ireland
Introductions Series and in 2014 he was nominated for a Hennessey New
Irish Writing Award.

Away

Sometimes there is only the scent
of sticklebacks over a seawall
and the buckling coastline to draw you
further into the ocean of yourself.

A heron plucks at a pile of seaweed.
The tide turns. Slavonian Grebes
plummet out of slate skies into
the churning sea. The rains holds.

You forget yourself in the salt-sweet
air, its inkling of dead crustaceans
and sex. Come night the moon

will be out to play among the rocks,
illuminating a thousand eyes,
and still you'll be far from home.

St Anne's Park, Sunday Morning

We come bleary-eyed, stumbling on a clearing
of the senses, the back-path of a wood
in which the sky leaks like pale blue flowers
through sun-shot leaves and webs of branches.
Odd how a felled tree trunk looks asleep
in the wildflowers that have sprung up all around it,
as if there were nowhere else for it to fall.
And there, where they've chopped another oak,
cut down rings of solid years – summer evenings,
winter storms – look how the river pulses by
the roots showing through the banks.
Our shadows get caught up in the moment,
run over centuries of stone so that what's left
is quick as sunlight balanced on our tongues.

Rosamund Taylor

was born in Dublin in 1989. In 2015, she was chosen to take part in the Poetry Introductions series run by Poetry Ireland, and gave a reading as part of the Dublin International Literature Festival. Her poems have appeared in magazines in both the UK and Ireland, including *Crannóg* and *The SHOp*. In 2012, she was short-listed for the Live Canon International Poetry Competition and for the Montreal International Poetry Prize in 2013. Last year her poem 'Between Cupar and Kirkcaldy' was nominated for a Pushcart Prize.

The Selkie's Wife

You don't hide my skin. You put it in your wardrobe
among floral dresses. It's greasy.

Pale, pale-eyed and cold, I'm uncanny,
looking human and moving wrong, hands held stiff

or fluttering around my face. Watching you
I see when to meet eyes, when to smile, and you

teach me to speak, the yes and the no. You let me hold
the no in my mouth for days.

Gentle, next to me, sleeping like any mammal, you're
soft, soft-faced, soft-muscled. I miss my teeth,

the carnivore's teeth I lost with my skin – now
I bruise red, but I want to crouch over you like a mother

hold your snores to my belly,
threaten the night with my grubby jaws.

And I want to be human. My skin in the wardrobe
grows stiff. Salt hardens the creases. You watch

as I hold it against a body limp with years
on the shore. I'm tired, I say.

Deep-eyed, quick, my throat long, I dive
into seaweed forests, grey holds me on all sides, this weight,

this weightlessness. Crushed and flying. I can't return
and I return to hang my skin among floral dresses.

Fossils

I find the dragon in the cave at the curve of the cliff
where samphire grows, caught but baring its teeth,

so many teeth, tangled like mouse tails,
creased wings distinct in stone. Listening to the slap

and suck of sea against shore, I pick a snakestone
from the banked sand, a snake frozen to a silvery coil,

headless, tail curled so close it vanishes. Someone took
a flashing adder, its tight fangs, made it cold, silvery,

silent. Could the same magic catch a dragon? Flying,
its liquid shadow on the waves, and the moment

after, silenced in mid-scream, the smoke
rising to nowhere, lost in the haze, and its cold drop –

as I fit the snakestone in my palm, I'm aching
to see the dragon fall, to know how.

NOTES FOR BROADSHEET POETS

Lindsey Holland

Writing from a Family Tree: Ghosts, Presences and Absences

The collection I'm writing draws on two years of research into my family tree. The poems aren't strictly about family history, nor about my ancestors in a factual way. I'm reminded of a point made by Hannah Lowe, commenting on her experiences of researching and writing her collection *Ormonde*: 'All I can do is emphasise that this is a work of fiction, with its origins in fact'. Genealogists depend on documented facts – they don't make up family trees, letting their imaginations roam – but most certificates and censuses reveal only very basic information: perhaps a name, address, date, age, occupation, relations or illnesses. How can such dry data become poetry?

For me, the poetry comes out of what's absent. The facts act as prompts and as a framework – they are necessary – but they're not enough on their own. Imagination will always rush to fill the gaps.

Your Place of Birth is a Question Mark

Let's begin with a bed, or at least with the premise of a bed:
a space prepared, whether mattress, wood or tiles,
with blankets, sheets or rags. The woman – a friend
or cousin – offers words, a steadied hand and a cloth wrung out
in the bowl or bucket where it drips and writhes.

She sees you crown. Her brown or blue eyes peer between
brunette, blonde or black hair, your mother's thighs'
anaemic white, or flushed, a bloodied North
through which her palms net you, little fish, in the gush
to this dark room, not large, not warm, no portraits,

chandeliers or garnitures are here. She looks through smoke
as the hearth breathes damp or crackles at her shins
and she licks at sweat. The doors of other families,
across the corridor, behind the wall, send ricochet
congratulations: a baby girl! Here, on this rectangle!

I've recently put together poems for a pamphlet, *Bloodlines*, which is the start of this work. It focuses on two generations of my maternal family: my great-great-grandmother, Catherine Stewart, and her son and daughter–in–law, John Stewart Mansfield and his wife Phoebe. I was haunted by Catherine. For over a year, I failed to find anything certain about her origins other than that she was from Scotland. I wasn't sure why but she gripped me. I was convinced I was overlooking something obvious. It became an obsession but throughout I was aware that I needed to begin writing poems. I wondered where I should draw the line: how long should I keep searching for Catherine's origins before enough was enough and I accepted that the facts were beyond my reach? I tried every trick to write about her. I made bubble charts. I wrote whilst meditating. I wrote whilst mostly asleep. I wrote the few facts I had as prose in case they sparked. I latched onto images: Catherine as a deer being hunted, Catherine in a smoky city. I wrote thousands of words about smoke and cut them up; they refused to form even a collage poem. Perhaps it was my own instinct speaking but whenever I tried to write I heard what seemed to be Catherine's voice insisting 'Not yet! *Find me first!*'. I'd return to the certificates and censuses, pursuing new ideas.

Part of the problem was that I couldn't decide on a mode of address for the poems. Writing first person narrative wasn't working because I didn't feel I knew Catherine's voice well enough; I couldn't become her. I wasn't able to write fluidly about her in the third person either because I couldn't see her. She was everywhere and nowhere. She might have grown up in a Perthshire valley, surrounded by greenery, and for a while I'd see her there. Then that Catherine would be replaced by a young woman in industrial Glasgow, and then again by a child paddling beside a loch. At one point I decided to write Catherine as a Legion-like character, allowing her to have various selves and histories. 'Don't write! *Find me first!*' was again the result and so I abandoned this approach too.

I wrote a couple of poems which seemed to be working. I read Fleur Adcock's collection *Glass Wings* around this time, and was struck by her use of second person narrative in some of the poems about probate records and wills. I began questioning Catherine and this discourse seemed to bring her to life a little. There was interaction. I'm wary of asking questions in poems but in this instance it felt right, perhaps because ironically the main fact was the uncertainty itself. Asking questions was an honest thing to do.

The Tagging: 1863, Greenock

A month before your sixth anniversary, and there you are
giving birth to your first. A long time to wait back then, wasn't it?
Most couples aimed for one a year and began
on their wedding night. Why did you wait?

Was it sickness? After all, this first child was born
with *Hydrocephalus*, fluid on the brain, a condition
which *'existed before birth and continued till death'*
according to her certificate.

You were staying with a cousin, Mary McFarlane,
at 7 Broad Close. It's gone now, the whole street has fallen
but even then it crumbled. In a photograph the walls are stained
and a gang of children, faster than the shutter, are ghosts already.

Did she help, this Mary, as the infant emerged? It must have been
a bloody hard labour. Did you cry, together, at the baby's efforts
to suckle? Or as you supported that head, the swollen scalp,
the body unready for the weight of it? You named the child

Elizabeth Stewart McFarlane Mansfield. A family
bible of names. Why did you tag her but none of her siblings?
For this brief creature, was a name all you could give? Did you consider
that I, Lindsey Mansfield Holland, your great-great-grandaughter
could find that record of our roots and thank you for it?

After almost a year of searching, I found my ghost. I had previously found
the birth and death certificates of her first child and knew from these that
she had a connection to Greenock, but now I knew she was born there, and
that her father was Irish and worked in a sugar factory. I knew her mother
had died early and that she was brought up by an aunt. I knew she worked
as a female servant for her sister's family, and that the sister died shortly
before Catherine moved to Liverpool to marry a seaman, my great-great-
grandfather. The poems poured out. Having certainties proved crucial. The
facts stood like rocks around which imagination flooded. It was possible
to animate scenes in the story and although the actions I described were
fictions, they were based on likely realities.

With all of my family history poems, these 'likely realities' have to be rich with detail. It's a conscious decision to imaginatively zoom in on these people's environments, filling them with the objects of everyday life. The big themes underpin each poem – writing about poverty in the nineteenth century will always involve births, illnesses, love, marriage, deaths, grief, stoicism perhaps – and I deliberately probe uncertainties – Keats's ideas about negative capability are important to me – but all of this would be abstract if it weren't first rooted in detail, in nouns. Basil Bunting advised 'Fear adjectives; they bleed nouns' and although he was making a point about language, the need is perhaps similar: ancestors are like adjectives – they are abstract, absences, they are ghosts – and too much of them will weaken a poem. They need to be tied down, given locations, homes, given nouns. I certainly can't write them any other way. I'm speaking very generally here and I'm aware that there are perhaps ways of writing family history poems which are abstract and placeless but effective. All I can say is that for me, at the time of writing this, it hasn't worked that way.

Solar Eclipse

18th July 1860

Carrion crows were the only birds
at ease on the strandline. The Mersey
was the grey of apocalypse
       but the marshes jittered with tiny,
       invisible hearts and songs
       of mutuality. You and he
were as far apart as those two bodies
above, glancing past each other,
two circles, entirely themselves,
       not even close, but appearing to nod.
       I see you, said the sun.
       I'm not afraid, said the moon.
If it were a magic trick,
they'd reach each other's furthest points
and instead of gliding on as you'd expected
       they'd chink together, somehow
       opening their metal, making gaps
       to slip through, linking, and then
they'd drop into a single ring,
the one behind the other, their whole
surfaces touching. You heard him then;

he said you weren't apart, that he saw you too.
You envied the birds' bravado: the way
they strutted, as if confident
you'd chink together, your bodies recalling
the trick, the sleight, dropping into place.

I was often aware of a sense of responsibility to these ancestors. Catherine grabbed me and seemed to insist that I tell her story 'truthfully' even though I knew that was ultimately impossible, but I didn't have ethical concerns when I wrote about her. None of my living relatives had any information about Catherine prior to my research. We didn't even know her name, although we had been told that her generation had 'come down from Scotland'. I felt more of an obligation to be fair to her son, John Stewart Mansfield, my great-grandfather. He was orphaned and I eventually found his orphanage admission papers in the Liverpool Central Library search rooms. If I relied solely on these documents, it would be easy to convey his early life as one of only struggle and loss, but in his case, stories have been passed down about his adventures and ideas. Some of these are quite important to my living relatives. He loved the Savoy operas. He cycled from Liverpool to London in the late 1890s. He loathed tenement housing and the way people lived 'one on top of the other'. I lacked these anecdotes about Catherine, and I lack them for other branches of my family too, but it is perhaps the job of the poet to imagine these realities when they are absent. Certificates and documents like orphanage records are in one sense illusions of fact: they will suggest that a person's life is a parade of key events: birth, baptism, grief, work, love, marriage, another birth, another death. But the truth of the person is perhaps their love of song, their politics, the objects they owned and loved, the undocumented adventures, the single phrase which might be passed down one generation, two, maybe only dying after the third. This is what's lost: the real person. Perhaps it's what Catherine really meant when she insisted that I find her.

Find Me First

For months, I'll hear you: 'Don't write. Not yet. *Find me first!*'
But what can I find? Not your facts and not your body,
although I'll cling to your ghost, although I'll hunt as hard
as you'll haunt me. There'll be no grave to visit.

I understand, although you cling to the bedroom
with all its echoes – the leak which drips from the beam
into the pan you also spit, hack, vomit and piss in,
the chat and clink of cooking downstairs, food you can't stomach,
the footsteps, creaks, and from the window a hubbub
of carts and washerwomen, the call of the rag-and-bone-man

I understand, although you cling to these moments
and to the memory of other sounds – the slosh and trickle
of the Clyde around your toddler toes, the hammering of iron
and the crack of steam, the thud of sugar sacks

I understand, although wheezing, you cling
to how your voice box worked, the way you'd twist
through trills like a Mistle Thrush, and would again if only
willpower were enough, if your lungs weren't carved into chunks

I understand, although you cling to smiles, and to the faces
of your children in the doorway, to impressions still warm
of their fingers on your arm, their eyes brimming in the window-light,
their bodies ready to run, you can tell, from this room
and all its shock, the reek, the greyness you've become

I understand, although you cling to names you've inhabited –
to Scotland, Renfrew, Greenock, Tatlock, Broad and Neptune,
to Market, Brook, Liverpool, Birkenhead, to the Mersey
and to each of their skies, to each cloud you ever saw
and to every ship, each shifting pocket of sun and rain
on stonework, grass, the varying river, always the water

I understand, although you cling, although you need to battle,
your blood needs ceasefire. Do you think it's been sufficient
to pass a love of song along, to cling to the torn
remnants of our roots, to Christian and clan names,
to tales and recipes, places, to speak of them enough
to reach me down the line, a century on, your blood still living?
I'll find you in all of this, before I write.

But I understand, although I see your blur and hear you now
you'll be unfound, lost bones, lost words, lost melody.
I understand that I am these things too.

David Kuhrt

The Common Good of the Word

Poetry: David Constantine (OUP, 2013)

This is an inspiring, intriguing, well-organised book, a most remarkable tribute to the importance of poetry in our lives. It abounds in really interesting and relevant eclectic examples, and detailed analysis of particular poems.

Poetry begins with impromptu conversation: before the formal construction of a poem is thought of, it grows from and thrives in the ordinary usage of a language. That both poetry and the ordinary usage it grows from are a joy to experience is exemplified in every line of David Constantine's *Poetry*. Should students of literature wonder how best to make use of its insights for their studies, Constantine's narrative on poetry, depending so little on the crossed 't's and dotted 'i's of theoretical analysis, is put in perspective by Ben Lerner's 'Poetry and why I dislike it' in his *New Statesman* 'Diary' of 18th June. A poet himself, although his conclusions corroborate Constantine's, Lerner's analytical rigour is taxing to digest. *Poetry*, by contrast, is a joy to read, which makes it an exceptional achievement.

Constantine points out what could be the hermetic nature of Englishness, and shows how, in his closing chapter, 'The Common Good', it is being enriched by cultural influences of poets who come from all over the world and then become English. Here he takes Seamus Heaney's collection *Human Chain* as an example of poetry which, appealing to 'necessary memory', provides 'links that connect us and ensure our humanity'. If it is from this particular 'common good', which Constantine puts his finger on with such acuity in his closing chapter, that English language poetry now must spring, let's see what we can learn about the actual composition of poetry, what it does and how it works, from his preceding chapters. I know of no other work on poetry which manages to describe it so broadly in the context of normative language use with so little reliance on academic method.

'Knowledge is partial. Poetry itself ... is abundant' says Constantine on the first page of his book (the Introduction), telling us: 'I can hope to say things about it, out of my own experience that readers will answer out of theirs'. Thus, instead of pedantry, we have, throughout the work, an eminently accessible, coherent narrative about poetry which derives, as he tells us to start with, from his school teacher's and fellow students' experience of what poetry is and does'. Words in fact being 'the common property of the tribe, at everyone's disposal... poetry depends for the saying on accepted conventions in order to question them', as Robert Graves does in his poem 'From the Embassy', where he 'calls the poet "an ambassador of Otherwhere"'.

Poetry takes time. In the first chapter, 'The Reading and Writing of Poetry', he refers to Goethe, who, speaking of some of his most celebrated ballads, tells us that 'he had carried them in him, gestating, for fifteen or twenty years'. His making of those poems 'was, whether rapid or very slow, a process of realization. It had gone on for hours or years with no, or only intermittent, conscious participation'. In the same chapter, taking comments of Brecht's about his writing of 'The Good Woman of Setzuan' as an example, Constantine explains that writing a poem is a process of realizing as much as possible the complex and immaterial matrix which constitutes its pre-existence. That matrix is the 'things unknown', which can't be known until they are bodied forth in forms. The 'airy nothing' only becomes something when by the act of writing it is given 'a local habitation and a name'. Later, referring to Brecht's materialist view of life and the 'airy nothing' of the inspiration that precedes the creation of a poem, he mentions Brecht's explicit conviction that 'the truth, however contradictory, many-faceted, fine and shifting it may be, must manifest itself concretely', and he quotes specific poems of Brecht's to illustrate the point. After all, as Blake said, poetry 'lives and moves' in 'minute particulars'; Carlos Williams, too, endorsed 'No ideas but in things', for, as Constantine stresses, 'every poem, like Antaeus, must keep at least one foot on the ground'.

Following a chapter on 'Translation', we get to chapter 3, 'The Good of It'. Here, after explaining why poetry gives pleasure without necessarily being pleasant, he concludes that 'Poetry won't stop the worst things happening. Against the always potentially lethal structures and mindset of a bureaucracy and a technology released from ethical controls nothing will help except the politics of a sceptical, critical, and eternally vigilant pluralism. But in the urgent business of fetching things so close that we are bound to see them, of particularising, naming, keeping things real and concrete, of making sure that the human being always has a face – in that very necessary undertaking, poetry will help'. It is, after all, 'unkillable, infinitely inventive, adapts to being able to deal with new realities, however vile'.

As in every chapter, Constantine quotes from and refers to a plethora of poets, with highly interesting and relevant snippets, too many to quote from. In this chapter alone, for example, Milton, Schiller, Coleridge, Keats, Owen, Rosenberg, Celan, Hardy, Kipling, Shakespeare, Goethe, Heaney, Dryden, Wordsworth, Pauline Stainer, Pound, Bunting, Whitman, Hopkins, W.H. Davies, Neruda, Milosz, Mandelstam, Akhmatova, Lowell, Lawrence,

Auden, Elizabeth Bishop, Herbert, R.S. Thomas..... and so on – all play their part, and inform the reader.

In chapter four, 'The Office of Poetry', he again confronts the issue of poetry as spokesman for our humanity in the particular and specific conditions of our varying lives together in society.

'Poetry, in my view, can do what the novel can', Constantine claims, as 'it offers life wholly'. After all, 'literature, and the arts altogether, are the chief means by which human beings attain to consciousness of their condition'. Referring to remarks Hardy makes in the preface to his *Poems of the Past and the Present* about 'unadjusted impressions', he asks: 'how does such a volume [of collected poetry] compete with the novel in telling life wholly? The total oeuvre of the poets, even if composed of only such slim volumes, may indeed amount to a whole in which "*all* things are given full play", the whole of the writer's life, the whole of his or her felt experience of the world. All lyric poems give glances of the whole of life, and their premise is always that the life they point to, touch on, glance off, in its entirety exceeds them'. Poetry, as opposed to literal description, is not definitive saying: it reads truthfully between lines.

In the course of this penultimate chapter, referring, *inter alia*, to Czeslaw Milosz, Lawrence, Larkin, Clare and (in the final section headed 'Saying the human') Novalis, he convinces us that 'By its very act, even in saying the worst, by its rhythms, by its beauty, by its tough and agile vitality, poetry asserts the hope of better. For there is no such thing as a nihilistic poem. Poets are makers: in the form of a poem, in beauty, they make sense'.

Optimistically, Constantine claims: 'Poetry has never been more various in its voices, its speakers, its *dramatis personae*, and so in its appeal. In Britain now we have a poetry beginning to be truly representative of the national mix – the classes, the races, the regions, the vernaculars, the conflicting interests, which greatly increases its power to help. Best of all, more women are writing and being published'.

This is a challenging, thought-provoking read, a vital handbook for students of poetry, their mentors and for poetry-lovers everywhere.

Ángel Crespo

Between the desired and desire

Who launches an arrow and does not go with it?
For where our desires go
there we go too, as the sun,
without leaving its sphere, burns us,
and as our glances are another means
of departing from ourselves.

Between the desired and desire
there are no distances, scarcely difference
— if the arrow goes straight to its destiny,
and even though it never reaches it.

Charles Tomlinson

B E T W E E N   T H E   D E S I R E D   A N D   D E S I R E
after the Spanish of Ángel Crespo

Who launches an arrow and does not go with it?
For where our desires go
there we go too, as the sun,
without leaving its sphere, burns us,
and as our glances are another means
of departing from ourselves.

Between the desired and desire
there are no distances, scarcely difference
-- if the arrow goes straight to its destiny,
and even though it never reaches it.

Note on Charles Tomlinson and Ángel Crespo

Though they were contemporaries and had many friends and literary acquaintances in common (most notably in Spain, Portugal and Italy), Ángel Crespo and Charles Tomlinson never met personally. Crespo died in Barcelona in December 1995, just months short of his seventieth birthday, after a life almost fully devoted to poetry, teaching and translation, and when Brenda and Charles Tomlinson travelled to Barcelona in April 1996 for a poetry reading, it was Pilar Gómez Bedate, Crespo's widow and a gifted scholar and translator in her own right, whom they met and befriended. Soon after, she sent them a copy of *Iniciación a la sombra* (*Induction to the Shadow*), Crespo's posthumous collection, most of whose poems had been written while in hospital.

Charles wrote back in early July acknowledging receipt of the book, praising the 'vividness and chastity of its writing', and adding: 'Who else could have written so purely and so firmly of this harrowing experience?' This was not mere courtesy. The book had made a deep impression on him and not long after he wrote a poem, 'In Memoriam Ángel Crespo' (*The Vineyard Above the Sea*, 1999), where the motif of the shadow is taken up and developed in his own fashion.

Agenda's Spanish issue, published in mid-1997 and guest-edited by myself, included nine poems by Crespo in English translations – three of them ('Just as the Blameless Beasts', 'Though I Ask the Air' and 'The Wick') by Charles. He must have translated 'Entre lo deseado y el deseo' ('Between the Desired and Desire') shortly afterwards, for he sent a longhand copy of his version to Pilar Gómez Bedate on November 1997.

Earlier this year I found the typescript of the poem in one of his letters to me. It was dated 29 January 2000 and came with the following suggestion: 'I wonder if the enclosed Crespo would be of use for the *Oxford Magazine*? (I've mislaid the Spanish text, should you need that). Don't forget we also have that version of de Sagarra's "Green Vines Above the Sea". Wouldn't they make a nice trio?'

This calls for a little explanation. At the time I was working as Language Assistant or *Lector* at Oxford University and had managed, quite implausibly, to place a couple of my own translations of English poems into Spanish in *Oxford Magazine*. Additionally, Charles is here referring to his version of Josep Maria de Sagarra's 'Vinyes verdes vora el mar', a lovely Catalan poem in the form of a popular ballad to which I'd drawn his attention as it addressed the same landscape that featured in the title poem of *The Vineyard Above the Sea*.

The third poem making up the 'nice trio' is his version of Manuel Altolaguirre's 'Las sombras', which was first published in *Oxford Magazine*, no. 178 (Second Week, Trinity Term 2000) and later in *Agenda*, vol. 40, no. 4.

As far as I'm aware, this version of Crespo's 'Entre lo deseado y el deseo' (from his 1985 book *El ave en su aire*) has not been published before. For some reason I don't recall – though it probably had to do with my coming back to Spain in 2000 – it was never sent to *Oxford Magazine* and languished among my papers.

In all these cases (and that goes also for the Crespo pieces he translated for *Agenda* back in 1997) I supplied him with a literal or line-by-line rendering of the original poem that he would then hammer and polish into English. I might add a short explanatory note, but I don't think he really needed it. He always managed to infuse the poems with his own personality – the elegance and suppleness of his poetic diction invariably giving them a new lease of life in English.

Jordi Doce

Biographies

Josephine Balmer's most recent collection is *The Word for Sorrow* (Salt). Previous collections and translations include *Chasing Catullus: Poems, Translations and Transgressions*, *Catullus: Poems of Love and Hate*, *Classical Women Poets* and *Sappho: Poems & Fragments*, all Bloodaxe. *Piecing Together the Fragments*, a study of classical translation and poetry, was published by Oxford University Press in 2013. A former chair of the Translators' Association, she is presently a judge of the Guardian/Stephen Spender Prize for poetry in translation. Her sonnet sequence, *Letting Go: Mourning Sonnets*, is to be published by *Agenda* Editions.

Mike Barlow's first collection *Living on the Difference* (Smith Doorstop, 2004) was overall winner of the Poetry Business Book and Pamphlet Competition and was shortlisted for the Aldeburgh Jerwood Prize for best first collection. A pamphlet, *Amicable Numbers* (Templar, 2008), was a Poetry Book Society pamphlet choice. His third collection is *Charmed Lives* (Smith/Doorstop, 2012). He won first prize in the 2006 National Poetry Competition.

William Bedford's selected poems, *Collecting Bottles Tops*, and selected short stories, *None of the Cadillacs Was Pink*, were both published in 2009. A new collection of poems, *The Fen Dancing*, was published in the spring of 2014. His poem 'Then' won First Prize in the 2014 Roundel Poetry Competition. His poem 'The Journey' won First Prize in the 2014 *London Magazine* International Poetry Competition.

Mara Bergman grew up in New York. Her poetry has been published widely and she is also the author of more than twenty books for young children. Her collection *The Tailor's Three Sons and Other New York Poems* won the 2014 *Mslexia* Poetry Pamphlet Competition. Mara lives in Tunbridge Wells, Kent. www. marabergman.com

Alison Brackenbury was born in Lincolnshire in 1953. Her latest collection is *Then* (Carcanet, 2013). Her ninth collection will be published by Carcanet in Spring 2016. Her poems can be heard online at the Poetry Archive, www.poetryarchive.org. New poems can be read at her website, www.alisonbrackenbury.co.uk

Carole Bromley teaches Creative Writing at York University. Twice a winner in the Poetry Business Book and Pamphlet Competition, she has two pamplets and a full length collection, *A Guided Tour of the Ice House (2012)*, with Smith/Doorstop. Carole has been published in magazines including *The Poetry Review, The North, The Rialto, Magma and Mslexia* and was recently commended in the Hippocrates Prize and shortlisted for the Manchester Prize for Writing for Children.

John F. Buckley currently lives in Orange County, California. His work has been published in a number of places, one of which nominated him for a Pushcart Prize in 2009. His chapbook *Breach Birth* was published on Propaganda Press in March 2011. His full-length collaboration with Martin Ott, *Poets' Guide to America*, is coming out on Brooklyn Arts Press in Summer 2012.

Vuyelwa Carlin was born in South Africa in 1949, brought up in Uganda, and read English at Bristol. She has had poems in many magazines, and four collections published to date (Seren), the latest being *The Solitary*, 2009. A fifth, *Long Shadows*, is to be published soon. She lives in Shropshire.

Martin Caseley has published two poetry collections with *Stride* and essays in *Agenda* and *PN Review*. He continues to work on autobiographical essays and poems on music and spirituality are forthcoming. He lives in Stamford, Lincolnshire and when not teaching, reviewing or reading, he spends time cycling and listening to unfashionable, forgotten rock music.

David Cooke's retrospective collection, *In the Distance*, was published in 2011 by Night Publishing. A new collection, *Work Horses*, was published by Ward Wood in 2012. His poems and reviews have appeared in journals such as *Agenda, The Bow Wow Shop, The Interpreter's House, The Irish Press, The London Magazine, Magma, The Morning Star, New Walk, The North, Poetry Ireland Review, Poetry Salzburg Review, The Reader, The SHOp and Stand*. He has two collections forthcoming: *A Murmuration* (Two Rivers Press, 2015) and *After Hours* (Cultured Llama Pres 2017).

Claire Crowther has published three full collections. The first, *Stretch of Closures*, was shortlisted for the Aldeburgh Best First Collection prize. She has also published four pamphlets. She is poet-in-residence for the Royal Mint during 2014-2015.

Martyn Crucefix's recent original collections include *Hurt* (Enitharmon, 2010), *The Time We Turned* (Shearsman, 2014), *A Hatfield* Mass (Worple Press, 2014). He has translated Rilke's *Duino Elegies* (Enitharmon, 2006) – shortlisted for the 2007 Popescu Prize for European Poetry Translation – and Rilke's *Sonnets to Orpheus* (Enitharmon, 2012). *Daodejing – a new version in English* will be published in 2016. For more visit www.martyncrucefix.com

Tony Curtis is emeritus Professor of Poetry at the University of South Wales where he introduced Creative Writing and ran the masters degree for two decades. He is currently Poet in Residence for the National Trust's Dyffryn Gardens in the Vale of Glamorgan. He takes his talk "My Life with Dylan Thomas " to the USA in September. His biog and publications are on www.tonycurtispoet@btinternet.com

Poet and verse translator, **Peter Dale**'s most recent books are: *Diffractions: New and Collected Poems* (Anvil Press) and *Local Habitation* (Anvil Press). His most reprinted translations are *Selected Poems of Francois Villon* and Dante's *Divine Comedy* in terza rima, both by Anvil Press. *Aquatints: New Poems 2012-2015* is reviewed in this issue.

Nicola Daly has had a number of poems published in magazines such as *The Rialto, Obsessed with pipework, Interpreters House, Magma, Envoi, The Flea, Myslexia* and *Southwords*. More recently two of her poems appeared in a Bloodaxe anthology entitled *Hallelujah for 50ft Women*.

Sue Davies was born in Lüneburg and grew up in London. She trained as a nurse practising at Westminster Hospital before going to work for BBC Radio at Broadcasting House. She married and lived in Oxford, and then moved with her husband to Cyprus. On her return, she studied English and Linguistics at the University of Sussex. She then lectured in English Literature at a Sixth Form College in Hampshire and for the Open University. She continues to live in Hampshire close to the sea, and has recently completed a fictionalised memoir. As a prize winning poet, she is now working on her second collection.

Alexandra Davis writes poetry while bringing up her four young sons and working as an English teacher. Born in Kent, she has lived in Suffolk for eighteen years with her husband after graduating from St Edmund's College, Cambridge. She has been published in *Agenda*, and was recently commended in the Second Light and Torriano competitions, as well as being a finalist in the Adlestrop Centenary competition last year. She also works as a Zumba instructor.

John F. Deane born Achill Island 1943; founded Poetry Ireland and *The Poetry Ireland Review*, 1979; Published several collections of poetry and some fiction; Won the O'Shaughnessy Award for Irish Poetry, the Marten Toonder Award for Literature, Golden Key Award from Serbia, Laudomia Bonanni Prize from L'Aquila, Italy. Shortlisted for both the T.S.Eliot prize and The Irish Times Poetry Now Award, won residencies in Bavaria, Monaco and Paris. He is a member of Aosdána. His recent poetry collection: *Snow falling on Chestnut Hill: New & Selected Poems* was published by Carcanet in October 2012. His latest fiction is a novel, *Where No Storms Come*, published by Blackstaff in 2010. A new collection of poems, *Semibreve*, has just been published by Carcanet in 2015 and a 'faith and poetry memoir', *Give Dust a Tongue*, has also been published by Columba this year. John F. Deane is Mayo County Council's Writer in Residence for 2015.

Terence Dooley has been published widely recently in magazines. He translates poetry and fiction from Spanish for the annual Spain Now festival. He is Penelope Fitzgerald's literary executor, and has edited her letters and essays.

Roger Elkin's poetry has won over 150 Prizes and Awards internationally, including the *Sylvia Plath Award for Poems about Women*. His published collections include *Blood Brothers, New & Selected Poems* (2006), *No Laughing Matter* (2007), *Dog's Eye View* (2009), and *Fixing Things* (2011). Editor of *Envoi* magazine, (1991-2006), he received the *Howard Sergeant Memorial Award for Services to Poetry*. A published critic on Ted Hughes, Roger tutors Poetry at Wedgwood College, Barlaston, and was shortlisted for the Keele University Poetry Prize (2007).

David Hale lives and works in Gloucestershire. His first *pamphlet, The Last Walking Stick Factory* was produced by Happenstance Press, his second, *In Bedlam's Wood* won the 2014 Templar Pamphlet competition. His first full collection is due from Templar later this year.

John Haynes won the Costa Prize in 2006, for his long poem *Letter to Patience*, the Troubadour Prize in 2007, and was shortlisted for the T S Eliot Prize in 2010 for another long poem, *You*. Further details in the *Oxford Companion to Modern Poetry*, and at jhaynestab.co.uk He spent most of his professional life lecturing at Ahmadu Bello University, Zaria, Nigeria, and now lives in Hampshire with his Nigerian-born wife and teaches for the WEA.

Wendy Holborow was born in South Wales, but lived in Greece for fourteen years where she founded and co-edited *Poetry Greece*. She has won prizes for short stories and poetry some of which have appeared in *Agenda, Envoi, Poetry Ireland Review, Poetry Salzburg Review, Roundyhouse*, and many others internationally. She is currently studying for a Masters in Creative Writing at Swansea University. Poetry Salzburg have recently published her pamphlet *After the Silent Phone Call* (2015). She is a member of the Literature Wales Writers of Wales database.

Lindsey Holland's small collection *Particle Soup* was published by KFS in 2012, and she is currently completing a full collection, *Bloodlines*, drawing on PhD research into family histories. She co-edits the online poetry magazine *The Compass* and she coordinates the regional network and publisher North West Poets. She lives in Aughton, Lancashire and has an MA in Writing from the University of Warwick. She teaches poetry at Edge Hill University. Twitter: @LindseyHolland

Danielle Hope was born in Lancashire, now lives in London, where she also works as a hospital doctor. She has had four collections of poems published: *Giraffe under a Grey Sky*, *Fairground of Madness*, *City Fox* and *The Stone Ship*, all by Rockingham Press. A fifth collection is being planned for 2015. Danielle was a trustee of Survivors Poetry for 5 years, is an editorial advisor to *Acumen*, and previously ran a magazine, *Zenos*, featuring British poetry and international poetry in translation. She previously edited a collection of poetry by Feyyaz Fergar (a notable Turkish poet and short story writer).

Roland John has had a long association with *Agenda*. *Agenda* Editions published his first full collection *Believing Words are Real* in 1985. He has written many articles and essays on Ezra Pound. His *A Beginner's Guide to The Cantos of Ezra Pound* examines each canto in detail. His latest poetry collection is *A Lament for England*. He is currently working on a new collection.

Tess Jolly (39) works part-time in a library and runs creative writing workshops for children. She has had work published in a wide range of magazines, including *Mslexia*, *Magma*, *The North*, *Agenda* and *Poetry News*.

Faye Joy studied Fine Art in the Midlands and continued to develop printmaking techniques at Central School of Art, London with Norman Ackroyd. She taught Art and History of Art as head of department for many years. Her last teaching post was at St Leonards-Mayfield School with her husband Paul. They retired to Normandy, France in 2005, since when Faye has concentrated on developing experimental machine embroidery work and, in recent years, poetry.

David Kuhrt is the author of *Wittgenstein the Tartar* on the epistemological errors of nominalism and positivism in Western philosophy (Academica Press 2013). He is also a painter – see the website www.kuhrtgallery.co.uk.

Tim Liardet has produced ten collections of poetry to date. His third collection *Competing with the Piano Tuner* was a Poetry Book Society Special Commendation and long-listed for the Whitbread Poetry Prize in 1998 and his fourth, *To the God of Rain*, a Poetry Book Society Recommendation for Spring 2003. *The Blood Choir*, his fifth collection, won an Arts Council England Writer's Award as a collection-in-progress, was a Poetry Book Society Recommendation, and shortlisted for the TS Eliot Prize for the best collection of the year. *Priest Skear*, a pamphlet, was the Poetry Book Society Pamphlet Choice for Winter 2010. *The Storm House*, his eighth full collection, appeared from Carcanet in July 2011. His tenth collection, *The World Before Snow*, appeared from Carcanet in March 2015; his *Arcimboldo's Bulldog: New and Selected Poems*, is due from Carcanet. He is Professor of Poetry at Bath Spa University.

Merryn Mac Carthy, has lived in South-West France since 2011. She is a retired Head of English and previously had her poems published by *The Irish Press*, *Agenda*, *Sussex University Press* and *English*, OUP. Her first full-length collection, *Playing Truant*, was published in 2010 by Agenda Editions. She lived previously in Southern Ireland, Devon and East Sussex.

Antony Mair lives in Hastings and is in the second year of a Creative Writing MA at the University of Lancaster. He has been previously published in *Agenda* and has also had poems accepted for publication in *Acumen*, *The Interpreter's House*, *Poetry Salzburg Review*, *Ink Sweat and Tears* and *The Lake*.

Maitreyabandhu has won the Keats-Shelley Prize, the Basil Bunting Award, and the Geoffrey Dearmer Prize. His debut collection, *The Crumb Road* (Bloodaxe, 2013) is a Poetry Book Society Recommendation. His new collection *Yarn* is forthcoming from Bloodaxe.

Rachel Mann is a priest in South Manchester. She is poet-in-residence at Manchester Cathedral and she is writing a PhD on fecundity and barrenness in 19th Century Women's Poetry.

Peter McDonald, born Belfast 1962, is a poet, scholar and critic. He is Professor of British and Irish Poetry, University of Oxford, and Christopher Tower Student and Tutor in Poetry in the English Language at Christ Church, Oxford. His *Collected Poems* came out from Carcanet in 2012.

Stuart Medland has written two collections of poems for children, composed whilst still a primary school teacher in Norfolk. Much of his writing is inspired by natural history and his large-format *Rings in the Shingle*, published by Brambleby Books, is a poetic celebration of Norfolk wildlife inspired by his own photographic encounters. *Ouzel on the Honister*, a volume of poems distilled from his many visits to the Lake District over the years, is currently in preparation. Stuart is now a regular contributor to *Agenda* and a collection of poems about his father, *Last Man Standing*, is currently available from *Agenda Editions*. He is presently engaged upon the second in the Norfolk wildlife series, to be entitled *The Worshipful Companies*.

W S Milne was born in Aberdeen in 1953. He has worked on *Agenda* for many years, and is now a trustee of the magazine. His play, *The Winter-Hoose*, based on the life of the Edinburgh poet, Robert Fergusson, has just been published by *Lallans* magazine.

Abegail Morley's new collection, *The Skin Diary* is forthcoming from Nine Arches Press (2016) and *The Memory of Water* – a collaboration with the artist Karen Dennison is due shortly from Indigo Dreams Publishing. Her debut collection, *How to Pour Madness into a Teacup* (Cinnamon 2009) was shortlisted for the Forward Prize Best First Collection, *Snow Child* (2011) and *Eva and George: Sketches in Pen and Brush (2013)* are published by Pindrop Press. She is currently Poet in Residence at Riverhill Himalayan Gardens, Kent and runs the website *The Poetry Shed*.

Ruth O'Callaghan, a Hawthornden fellow, has been translated into six languages and has read extensively in Asia, Europe and the USA. In 2010 she was awarded a gold medal for her poetry. She is a competition adjudicator, interviewer, reviewer, editor, workshop leader and mentor. Her sixth collection *An Unfinished Sufficiency* is due to be published in 2015.

Jeremy Page is the founding editor of *The Frogmore Papers*. He lives in Lewes, East Sussex, and teaches at the University of Sussex. His first full collection of poems *The Alternative Version* was published in 2001 and his second *Closing Time* appeared from Pindrop Press in 2014. His translations of Catullus's Lesbia poems have been published by Ashley Press as *The Cost of All Desire*.

Nigel Prentice has had work published over a number of years in various journals, including *Poetry Review*, *The London Magazine*, *The Rialto*, *Long Poem Magazine* and *Agenda*. He won the Rialto/RSPB Nature Poetry Competition 2015.

Stuart Pickford teaches in a comprehensive school in Harrogate.

Sheenagh Pugh now lives in Shetland, but lived for many years in Wales. She has published 12 collections with Seren, including a *Selected Poems* and a *Later Selected*. Her current collection is *Short Days, Long Shadows* (Seren 2014).

Omar Sabbagh is a widely published poet and critic. Two of his extant collections are: *My Only Ever Oedipal Complaint* and *The Square Root of Beirut* (Cinnamon Press, 2010/12); a fourth collection: *To The Middle of Love* is forthcoming with Cinnamon in winter 2016/17. His Beirut novella, *Via Negativa: A Parable of Exile* is released by Liquorice Fish Books near the start of 2016. He has published, in academic mode, or more belle-lettristic, on George Eliot, Ford Madox Ford, G.K. Chesterton, Robert Browning, Henry Miller, Lawrence Durrell, Joseph Conrad, and others; as well as many contemporary poets. He now teaches at the American University in Dubai (AUD). www.omarsabbagh.me.

Caroline Smith has published two poetry books with Flambard Press. *Flambard New Poets1* and *Thistles of the Hesperides*. She is currently finishing her new collection, *The Immigration Handbook*. Her poems have been widely published in journals including the Bloodaxe anthology *Staying Alive*. Her poetry has been set to music and performed by the BBC Singers on Radio 3. In 2012 and 2013 she was a prize-winner in the Troubadour Poetry Competition. She works as the Immigration and Asylum caseworker for a London MP.

Beth Somerford lives in Brighton with her composer husband and has four grown up children. She acts and directs, and also runs a small pottery. Beth Somerford has had a poems in a number of publications. She was first runner up in the Frogmore Prize in 2014. Beth's alter ego, Sam Chittenden, is Director of the creative training company Different Development, and author of *Rhyme & Reason: The Poetry of Leadership*.

Seán Street has published nine collections, his latest being *Cello* (Rockingham Press, 2013) and *Jazz Time* (Lapwing Publications, 2014). Prose includes *The Poetry of Radio* (Routledge, 2013) and *The Memory of Sound* (Routledge, 2015). Other works include *The Wreck of the Deutschland* (Souvenir Press, 1992) and *The Dymock Poets* (Seren, new edition, 2014). He broadcasts radio features and documentaries on Radios 3 and 4.

Rosita Sweetman lives in Ireland. The Lilliput Press in Dublin republished her 1972 novel, *Fathers Come First* as a modern classic last year. Lilliput are due to publish her latest novel, *Chronic Love*, this year, and plan to also republish her 1970's classics, *On Our Knees* and *On Our Backs*. She's part of the *Mauvaise Graine*, New Anthology of 21st Century Irish Poets launched this year. She has worked in Africa, Sri Lanka, Bangladesh, South America.

Colin Wilcockson graduated in English Language & Literature at Merton College, Oxford. He was elected to a Fellowship at Pembroke College, Cambridge, where he was for many years Director of Studies in English and in Anglo-Saxon, Norse & Celtic. He is now an Emeritus Fellow. He has published books, articles and reviews, mainly on Medieval literature (he is one of the editors of *The Riverside Chaucer*, and recently produced an edition of *The Canterbury Tales* with facing-page translation for Penguin.) He also writes on David Jones.

Dylan Willoughby has received fellowships from Yaddo and The MacDowell Colony. His poetry has appeared in *Agenda*, *Stand*, and elsewhere, and Chester Creek Press has published a limited edition chapbook, *Dusk at St. Mark's*.

Christian Wiman is the author of numerous books of poetry, prose, and translations. From 2003 until 2013 he was editor of *Poetry* magazine in Chicago. He now teaches at the Yale Institute of Sacred Music.

Visit www.agendapoetry.co.uk

Book store, news, Agenda events, sound-bites

Online Broadsheet 26 for young poets and artists

and

Web supplement:

Essays:

Arthur Broomfield:
The Letters of Samuel Beckett 1957-1967

David Cooke:
A Grafted Tongue: Louis de Paor

Patricia McCarthy:
Peripatetic Poets: **Nessa O'Mahony**
Sarah Berkeley Tolchin and
Sarah Maguire

Poems:
More poetry from poets in this issue, as well as:

Christine McNeill	**Liz Barton**
Isabel Bermudez	**Omar Sabbagh**
John Gladwell	**Paul McMahon**
Karl O'Hanlon	**Polly East**
Laura Corraducci	**Simon Jenner**
Terese Coe	**Rosalynde Price**

Featured artist:
Brenda Hartill RE

Don't forget to sign up for our free e-newsletter (scroll down your Agenda email and sign up).

AGENDA Poetry Festival

16th and 17th October 2015

Download the programme at **www.agendapoetry.co.uk**

MAYFIELD SCHOOL

Mayfield School hosts the

AGENDA
POETRY FESTIVAL

16th & 17th October 2015

FEATURING
INTERNATIONALLY
CELEBRATED POETS

PATIENCE AGBABI

DALJIT NAGRA

MIMI KHALVATI

GRACE NICHOLS

TIMOTHY ADÈS

ROBIN ROBERTSON

PATRICIA MCCARTHY

DAVID POLLARD

POETRY WORKSHOPS & PERFORMANCES BY POETS AND MAYFIELD STUDENTS

Mayfield School, The Old Palace, Mayfield, East Sussex TN20 6PH
Booking office: 01435 874600   Email: enquiry@mayfieldgirls.org

To be launched in

AGENDA Poetry Festival

Mayfield, East Sussex

- This 'Family Histories' issue of *Agenda*

- David Pollard's *Finis-terre* (Agenda Editions), described by W S Milne as 'a very impressive long poem, somewhat akin to Eliot's *Four Quartets*. Internalised images and classical allusions are used to great effect, along with a clever play on words and painterly colour – all with so many layers and levels of meaning'.

and

- Patricia McCarthy's *Letters to Akhmatova* (Waterloo Press/Agenda Editions) about which Elaine Feinstein, Akhmatova's translator and biographer, commented: 'Such moving, insightful lyrics in these lovely *Letters to Akhmatova*.... and what an ear Patricia McCarthy has for melody!'

Finis-terre
David Pollard
with an introduction by Jason M. Wirth

Letters to Akhmatova
Patricia McCarthy

Both books are available in Agenda's online bookshop:

www.agendapoetry.co.uk

THEPOETRYSOCIETY

Presents

National Poetry Competition

Judges: Sarah Howe
Esther Morgan
David Wheatley
Deadline: 31 Oct 2015

First prize: £5000
Second prize: £2000
Third prize: £1000
Commendations: £200

**It's easy to enter online at www.poetrysociety.org.uk/npc
or call us on 020 7420 9880 for more information**